ACTS 29ERS INTERNATIONAL:
&
'POINT 2 POINT WITH JESUS:'

"FOUNDATIONS FOR CHRISTIAN LIVING."

BARRIE J. ROWLAND-HORNBLOW:
PASTOR ('RE-TYRED')

"A CALEB PUBLICATION"

Copyright © 2024 by Ps. Barrie Rowland-Hornblow

All rights reserved. No part of this book may be reproduced in any manner whatsoever without the express written permission of the publisher except in the case of brief quotations in a book review or scholarly journal.

First printing: 2024

ISBN: 978-0-6459827-2-5

A Caleb Publication.

Other books under the cover of 'Point 2 Point with Jesus Ministries' are:
'Living In Faith.'
'Our God of Common-Sense.'
'Living In the Way, the Truth, and the Life.'
'Walking In the Light of God's Word.'
'Foundation for Christian Living.'

"THROUGH WHICH A CHRISTIAN CAN EXPLORE THE TRUTHS OF GOD'S PLAN FOR HIS PEOPLE:"

"Point 2 Point with Jesus Ministry" is an affiliate 'not for profit' division of the Acts 29ers International Ministries." And includes series of studies and books which have been brought together to help bring an awareness of the beauty found within the Word of God.

Pastor Barrie and can be contacted for any expressions of interest in their Teaching / Preaching ministry through the offices of:

Acts 29ers International
&
'Point 2 Point with Jesus Ministry.

Email: pastorbarrie@gmail.com

www.point2pointwithjesus.com

All Scripture is taken from 'The Message' translation unless otherwise designated.

Choruses are those that have personally impacted my life and are ones that I love to sing. Most of them are in the 'Praise and Worship' of The Resource Song Book. (Arranged by Nolene Prince and produced by Resource Christian Music.) I have given credit to the authors where indicated and Glory to God for all others.

Wherever indicated by the * the reader may be able to gain something to remember that, just as I have found, God will impress upon us things that through the years, become a part of who we are IN HIM.

Content:

FINDING OUR FOUNDATION.	11:
LEARNING TO TURN AROUND.	30:
WHAT IS THE BASIS FOR REPENTANCE.	46:
PREPARING THE WAY OF THE LORD.	75:
BECOMING FULLY PERSUADED.	103:
FAITH IS FOUNDED UPON FACT	137:
THE RIGHTEOUSNESS OF FAITH	154:
FAITH THAT WORKS	180:
REDEMPTION THROUGH FAITH IN HIS BLOOD.	204:
NOW IS THE ONLY TIME WE HAVE WITH JESUS.	226:
BEGNNING A NEW LIFE IN JESUS	253:
FULFILLING ALL RIGHTEOUSNESS.	267:
QUOTABLE QUOTES FOR YOU.	285:

In presenting this my fifth book 'Foundation for Christian Living' I would like to continue to dedicate its contents to the wonderful people of Sri Lanka, who have over the past eighteen years adopted me into their respective fellowships and assemblies and have embraced, with me, the concept of becoming "ACTs 29ers International."

Although I continue to be involved in Acts 29ers International we have, in 2022, invited Ps. Victor Soo, founder of the REACH Family Church in Northcote, Victoria to take the leadership role in regard to the Sri Lankan areas of ministry from July 2022. He has been nominally heading this work for the past eighteen months and it was time for me to release this work into his most capable hands.

However, it is my special privilege to thank the many Pastor's wives and families who have cared for me and shared the 'family space' which I recognize as so important within their respective homes. You can be assured that Noelene and I, would love the honour of returning your gift of hospitality should you come to visit us in Australia.

Pastor Barrie
Executive Director of Ministry
Acts 29ers International. A.C.M.I. (Sri Lanka)
www. Point2pointwithjesus.com

TRIBUTES:

I take this opportunity to thank my wife Noelene for her supporting faith in this my 'Journey of obedience' to the Holy Spirit of God. Such a journey, that without her loyalty and prayerful support, I would not be able to undertake such as the Lord has willed for me.

Also, to a very good friend – who has gone to that Eternal place of blessing – Lorraine Dickman who was my Church Secretary in the Living Waters Family Church in Frankston Victoria. Lorraine had a natural love for Sri Lanka and its people because she is Sri Lankan by birth. After the 2004 Tsunami, Lorraine encouraged me to go to Mampitiya in the Southern Province to help her friend Pastor Nandasena. The rest of the story is written in Acts 29ers history, and the hearts of the Sri Lankan people.

Also, to the assemblies who have given of their time and substance to sustain me over the many years whilst I have been ministering in Australia, India, and for the past seventeen years in Sri Lanka. The Frankston "Living Waters Family Church," the "Mornington C.R.C.," the "Ararat Church of Christ" each have gone beyond their own "Mission Field" to give me both financial and prayerful support over the life of Acts 29ers. And the congregation of the 'Eternity' church in Morwell, who sent a four-person team with me in 2017. Not forgetting the wonderful individuals, each of whom have with both their prayer and financial support enabled the commitments to be undertaken and met each ministry trip, year upon year.

To all of you I accept the honour and the responsibilities of serving the Body of Christ, so that HIS Name shall be glorified, and the borders of HIS tent shall be enlarged by the gathering in of Souls, into HIS KINGDOM.

P. B.

Thank you for purchasing 'Foundation for Christian Living' and it is my fervent hope – anticipated expectation – that you like it and prayerfully gain something from its pages.

'Acts 29ers International' and 'Point 2 Point with Jesus Ministry' are dedicated to raise ministries wherever God directs. To do this we need funding and respectfully ask you the reader to consider giving support through donations either monthly, annually or as a one-off gifting, so that we can support such potential ministries and equip them for service.

All the above-mentioned books and others to follow, will help service the "Core" working of our ministry. All finances gained from the purchase of this, and other Point 2 Point enterprises are sown into the work of Acts 29ers International Ministries, an affiliated member with both the ACM and ACMI accredited Christian Bodies.

Our bank details for donations are as follows:
Acts29ers International BSB 633 000
Account Number 134 201 508.

The Lord has extended to me His favour in the writing of these books, and I dare to believe, that there is a three-fold purpose in His doing so.

1. To stretch our growing in Him:
2. To enable His work, in places and peoples with whom I have been connected in ministry over the past 49years of service, to continue.
3. To bless you the reader and thereby to encourage you – the reader – to be stretched in that which He may 'call you' to become involved.

Dedication:

This book is, by way of thanks and appreciation, dedicated to the leaders of the New Life Christian Centre in Moe Victoria. Pastors. Lyle Potts, Bruce Gilding, Barrie Ryan, Ian Edwards, and of course to all those who had to put up with me in those earlier years 1974 -1981, when I was still 'a little bit wet behind the ears', and asked so many questions, so to speak.

The fact that I came to the Lord and worshipped among them, in 1974, married my wife Noelene in 1977, and was ordained within the Christian Revival Crusade in 1979, means that I can say, with confidence, that those leaders and members of the Moe New Life Centre influenced my future years in His service. Thank you, and may God continue to work the works of outreach which were for all of us a measure of our willingness to follow His pathway both in witness and testimony.

Together with my wife Noelene we have been involved in direct Christian service in Victoria – Moe and the Latrobe Valley, Frankston, and Mornington, in Tasmania – Launceston and, Wynyard; West Australia – Bull Creek, Freemantle, Laverton, Karratha, Beverley, Gosnell, Perth, Geraldton, Armadale, and the T.S. Canning RAN Reserve, as Chaplain.

In 1991 we were called to Frankston Victoria, where we were privileged to raise 'The Living Waters Family Church' of which this current book speaks of how God raised up a team of Believers. And in 1998 Pastor Hal Oxley invited my wife Noelene, and myself, to join Associated Christian Ministries A.C.M. and we are credentialled within that covering.

It was from the base in Frankston that God encouraged me to go to Sri Lanka, and from 2005/2022 to raise up Acts 29ers International Ministries which is affiliated with A.C.M.I.

We can report with joy, that during a nineteen-year period, God has strengthened four existing Church fellowships. And He has provided the inspiration to raise some 27 Indigenous young men and women to become leaders in an outreach program which to this date have raised 9 new assemblies – and still counting – of believers throughout the beautiful country of Sri Lanka.

And now in 2024 we are commencing a new journey The Holy Spirit charged me to reveal Jesus to all who would hear His voice and thereby respond to His call upon their lives, to live right with God and also to live right with their fellow humans in the community.

Although I turned 86 years old in April 2024, I believe God will continue to lead me along His pathway with both His Lamp to guard in the present time and His Light to show me the path forward to where He desires me to be. Psalm 119 verse 105;

Pastor Barrie.

Chapter 1:

"FINDING OUR FOUNDATION"

Luke 6:31-49; *"Here is a simple rule of thumb for behavior: Ask yourself what you want people to do for you; then grab the initiative and do it for them! If you only love the lovable, do you expect a pat on the back? Run-of-the-mill sinners do that.*

If you only help those who help you, do you expect a medal? Garden-variety sinners do that. If you only give for what you hope to get out of it, do you think that's charity? The stingiest of pawnbrokers does that. "I tell you, love your enemies. Help and give without expecting a return.

The key to understanding Scripture is in understanding that – God the Author – is the utmost 'Common-Sense Communicator' of all time. *(book 2 'Our God of Commonsense')*

You'll never—I promise—regret it. Live out this God-created identity the way our Father lives toward us, generously and graciously, even when we're at our worst. Our Father is kind; you be kind.

"Don't pick on people, jump on their failures, criticize their faults—unless, of course, you want the same treatment. Don't condemn those who are down; that hardness can boomerang.

Be easy on people; you'll find life a lot easier. Give away your life; you'll find life given back, but not merely given back—given back with bonus and blessing. Giving, not getting, is the way. Generosity begets generosity.

Remember that it easier to smile, to be generous, to be kind and to have compassion than it is to frown, to be miserly, to hate or to have revenge: So, have consideration of who you are and who God says you are – in Him – than what the devil says about you.

He quoted a proverb: 'Can a blind man guide a blind man?' Wouldn't they both end up in the ditch? An apprentice doesn't lecture the master. The point is to be careful who you follow as your teacher. "It's easy to see a smudge on your neighbor's face and be oblivious to the ugly sneer on your own. Do you have the nerve to say, 'Let me wash your face for you,' when your own face is distorted by contempt? It's this I-know-better-than-you mentality again, playing a holier-than-thou part instead of just living your own part.

A good example was given to me when listening to a congregant telling me with such forthright – earnest – intent, about her struggle to do what she believed was her duty.

The word God spoke into my spirit was that she must understand that God desired for her to be, in that Godly Commonsense attitude and not to strive:
'JUST BE.'

Wipe that ugly sneer off your own face and you might be fit to offer a washcloth to your neighbor. "You don't get *wormy apples off a healthy tree, nor good apples off a diseased tree. The health of the apple tells the health of the tree. You must begin with your own life-giving lives.*

Understanding God's Love and purpose for all He has done is best understood when we consider the garden. When we attend to the nurturing of the Garden in which we have planted the fruit, or in my case the rose garden, we consider the type of soil and the condition of the plant, to attend to the colour of the inside of the house is not relevant to the state of our garden plant, although if the fruit or the flower is not healthy it will affect our health on the inside won't it.

It's who you are, not what you say and do, that counts. Your true being brims over into true words and deeds. "Why are you so polite with me, always saying, 'Yes, sir,' and 'That's right, sir,' but never doing a thing I tell you?

These words I speak to you are not mere additions to your life, homeowner improvements to your standard of living. They are foundation words, words to build a life on. If you work the words into your life, you are like a smart carpenter who dug deep and laid the foundation of his house on bedrock. When the river burst its banks and crashed against the house, nothing could shake it; it was built to last.

But if you just use my words in Bible studies and don't work them into your life, you are like a dumb carpenter who built a house but skipped the foundation. When the swollen river came crashing in, it collapsed like a house of cards. It was a total loss."

Remember; We, are God's ambassador to all those we encounter. God will give us the things to say, but we must be 'living epistles' in our daily life and the living of it, as we speak out the Gospel message.

Hebrews 6:1-3; *"So come on, let's leave the preschool finger-painting exercises on Christ and get on with the grand work of art. Grow up in Christ.*

The basic foundational truths are in place: turning your back on "salvation by self-help" and turning in trust toward God; baptismal instructions; laying on of hands; resurrection of the dead; eternal judgment". "God helping us, we'll stay true to all that. But there's so much more. Let's get on with it!"

Babies belong in prams. Children belong in school. Adults belong in the working marketplace of living. We must follow God's guiding Light and become who we are according to His plan and make His plan our plan. Let us therefore get on with it.

The term "foundation" has been borrowed from the language of building and architecture. It refers to the very first thing we do in building - we prepare a solid stable support for the superstructure.

Since the foundation must carry the weight of the entire building, it must be done well. More than one building has

sagged or fallen because of a poor foundation. The taller the building is to be, the deeper the foundation.
Remember that we are discussing the biggest building the world has ever seen.

Spiritually speaking, the foundation is the basis of Christian doctrine and experience – and these two are never separate – upon which all other later development depends.

Hebrews 11:1-3; *"The fundamental fact of existence is that this trust in God, this faith, is the firm foundation under everything that makes life worth living. It's our handle on what we can't see. The act of faith is what distinguished our ancestors, set them above the crowd. By faith, we see the world called into existence by God's word, WHAT WE SEE CREATED BY WHAT WE DON'T SEE."*

The term "foundation stones" is used to help us emphasize the distinction of each truth to be both believed and experienced. Christ Himself is the only foundation which can be laid, and we enter into His foundation through our practical experience and specific encounters with Him, in obedient faith.

We are built upon the foundation, which is Christ, by the Holy Spirit, and through the ministry of those who labour with God.

1Corinthians 3:5-17; *"Who do you think Paul is, anyway? Or Apollos, for that matter? Servants, both of us—servants who waited on you as you gradually learned* to entrust your lives to our mutual Master. We each carried out our servant assignment. I planted the seed, Apollos watered the plants, but God made you grow.

When the importance of the speaker – messenger – becomes greater than the message we will have gone beyond our used by date and need to change our position or step away from getting in the way of the message.

It's not the one who plants or the one who waters who is at the centre of this process but God, who makes things grow. Planting and watering are menial servant jobs at minimum wages. What makes them worth doing is the God we are serving. You happen to be God's field in which we are working. Or, to put it another way, you are God's house.

Using the gift God gave me as a good architect, I designed blueprints; Apollos is putting up the walls. Let each carpenter who comes on the job take care to build on the foundation! Remember, there is only one foundation, the one already laid: Jesus Christ.

Take particular care in picking out your building materials. Eventually there is going to be an inspection. If you use cheap or inferior materials, you'll be found out. The inspection will be thorough and rigorous. You won't get by with a thing.

If your work passes inspection, fine; if it doesn't, your part of the building will be torn out and started over. But you won't be torn out; you'll survive—but just barely.

You realize, don't you, that you are the temple of God, and God himself is present in you? No one will get by with vandalizing God's temple, you can be sure of that. God's temple is sacred—and you, remember, are the temple."

The foundational doctrines were brought to us through the apostles and prophets who received the inspired Scriptures through the Holy Spirit, and by those same special words and anointing given to them He has also given us by God, Who created us by His power, to be His people.

Ephesians 2:16-22; *"Christ brought us together through his death on the Cross. The Cross got us to embrace, and that was the end of the hostility. Christ came and preached peace to you outsiders and peace to us insiders.*

He treated us as equals, and so made us equals. Through him we both share the same Spirit and have equal access to the Father. That's plain enough, isn't it? You're no longer wandering exiles.

What I can say with personal assurance is that my journey B.C. *(before I found Christ)* was tormented by the fact that I had no personal identity to hang my name upon. My early life was as a 'war orphan' without any knowledge of who my parents were. So, with no knowledge of family or heritage, and without a history, so to speak, I had come to believe that I had no future, and because I had neither of these essential ingredients, I felt that I had no hope either.
(From the Australian perspective liken to the "Stolen Generation.)

Since the advent of my new life in Christ, I have found my identity and therefore have accepted with joy a destiny that I believe God – my heavenly Father – gave me in the beginning.

This kingdom of faith is now your home country. You're no longer strangers or outsiders. You belong here, with as much right to the name Christian as anyone. God is building a home. He's using us all—irrespective of how we got here—in what he is building. He used the apostles and prophets for the foundation.

Even though I have made 'simple' that early life embracing those first 37 years, it is the ongoing foundational teaching over the past 46 years, which has enlightened me to be who I have become today.

Now he's using you, fitting you in brick by brick, stone by stone, with Christ Jesus as the cornerstone that holds all the parts together. We see it taking shape day after day—a holy temple built by God, all of us built into it, a temple in which God is quite at home."

As God's Word becomes our foundation through both teaching and experience, we are able to worship and find our place in His Church.

1 Peter 2:9-13; *"But you are the ones chosen by God, chosen for the high calling of priestly work, chosen to be a holy people, God's instruments to do his work and speak out for him, to tell others of the night-and-day*

difference he made for you – from – nothing to something, from rejected to accepted.

It was when reflecting – on a trip to Tasmania in company with Pastor Lyall Potts – upon how I became a Christian that I was drawn to the story of Isaiah and how he began his journey in the service of God. This is how I found the reality and purpose of my living out of this call to ministry, to which I have personally been called, and I have adopted the example – in a manner of speaking – of Isaiah 6:1-9; as the framework within which I can boldly live out my personal testimony.

Isaiah 6:1-9; (NKJV) "In the year that King Uzziah died, I saw the Lord sitting on a throne, high and lifted up, and the train of His robe filled the temple. above it stood seraphim; each one had six wings: with two he covered his face, with two he covered his feet, and with two he flew.

And one cried to another and said: "Holy, holy, holy is the LORD of hosts; The whole earth is full of His glory!" And the posts of the door were shaken by the voice of him who cried out, and the house was filled with smoke.

So, I said: "Woe is me, for I am undone! Because I am a man of unclean lips, And I dwell in the midst of a people of unclean lips; For my eyes have seen the King, The LORD of hosts."

Then one of the seraphim flew to me, having in his hand a live coal which he had taken with the tongs from the altar. And he touched my mouth with it, and said: "Behold, this has touched your lips; Your iniquity is taken away, And your sin purged."

Also, I heard the voice of the Lord, saying: "Whom shall I send, And who will go for Us?" Then I said, "Here am I! Send me." "And He said, "Go, and tell this people:"

(Continuing:) 1 Peter 2 9-13; *Friends, this world is not your home, so don't make yourselves cozy in it. Don't indulge your ego at the expense of your soul. Live an exemplary life among the natives so that your actions will refute their prejudices. Then they'll be won over to God's side and be there to join in the celebration when he arrives. Make the Master proud of you by being good citizens. Respect the authorities, whatever their level."*

The worldly-wise masons rejected the cornerstone because it was a different shape from all other stones. It did not seem to fit into any of the usual places.

This is a picture of the Jews rejecting their Messiah because he did not fit their expectations. It is also a picture of much of modern theology, which has no place for a living Lord, who will define his own truth in terms of life-transforming experience.

The first principles – foundation stones – too often will not fit our neat little traditions. So, as we begin building – with these foundation stones of God's Word – we must start all over from the beginning.

The letter to the Hebrews lists six basic foundational truths we must have with Christ, before we are brought to maturity in Him. The Holy Spirit, God's building inspector, will not give us a "building permit" to erect the edifice until he finds our foundations ready.1. Repentance from dead works: 2. Faith toward God: 3. Doctrine of baptisms: 4. The Laying on of hands: 5. Resurrection of the dead: 6. Eternal judgment:

Leaving the principles of the doctrine of Christ means literally to go on from the beginning. We are not to stop and constantly review the first elementary truths we learnt in Christ. We must leave them – not in the sense of forgetting them but in the sense of using them as a firm grounding underneath us – as we go on to higher truths.

We no longer need to recite our three time's table to know that 3x4=12. The smart equation is simply put. And it is the K.I.S.S. principle: * 'Keep It Short And Simple.'

Once again may we be reminded of the God whom we identify as our Creator. He is our God of the Common-sense. (the title of my second book. September 2021)

We are confident that the higher truths can be reached and held – not if – but when, we have established a firm foundation. This foundation is made sure as we have come to know the Lord in these areas, and it is then that we stand firm when the storms of life beat against us, and they most assuredly will. A chorus I learnt as a new Christian 1974 and still enjoy singing to this very day is:

> *"Being confident of this very thing,
> that He who has begun a good work in you
> will perform it until the day of Jesus Christ".*
> *Pamela Greenwood: from Phil 1:6; K.J:*

* 'Failing To Put Into Practice What We Have Heard From God Is Fooling Ourselves. We Will Have To Give Account Of What We Did With Everything We Heard.'

If we make a habit of not really doing what we are told, we soon become lawless and eventually will be called "workers of iniquity or lawlessness."

If we make a habit of not really listening, we will lose the power to hear. So that when the storm comes - and it does in every life – *'We will not be able to stand.'*

God tests our submission to His Lordship on the basis of our obedience to His instructions concerning these foundations, and also that these foundation stones and the laying of them are not optional but a Divine command.

This passage of Scripture has become perhaps the defining expression of all I need in Jesus, because it lays out clearly the map from which – for me personally – all direction is given as I need it, and when the timing is God's – not mine – to dictate.

Matthew 7:12-23; *"Here is a simple, rule-of-thumb guide for behaviour: Ask yourself what you want people to do for you, then grab the initiative and do it for them. Add up God's Law and Prophets and this is what you get.*

"Don't look for shortcuts to God. The market is flooded with sure-fire, easy-going formulas for a successful life that can be practiced in your spare time. Don't fall for that stuff, even though crowds of people do.

The way to life—to God! —is vigorous and requires total attention. Be wary of false preachers who smile a lot, dripping with practiced sincerity. Chances are they are out to rip you off some way or other. Don't be impressed with charisma; look for character. Who preachers are, is the main thing, not what they say. A genuine leader will never exploit your emotions or your pocketbook. These diseased trees with their bad apples are going to be chopped down and burned.

Knowing the correct password—saying 'Master, Master,' for instance—isn't going to get you anywhere with me. What is required is serious obedience—doing what my Father wills.

I can see it now—at the Final Judgment thousands strutting up to me and saying, 'Master, we preached the Message, we bashed the demons, our God-sponsored projects had everyone talking.' And do you know what I am going to say? 'You missed the boat.

All you did was use me to make yourselves important. You don't impress me one bit. You're out of here."

As believers we should never be alone because we have become part of God's people - His Church - by looking to Christ, through those foundational experiences common to

23

all genuine seekers of a meaning relationship with their Creator and Father.

Isaiah 28:16; Amplified: *"Therefore says the Lord God, 'Behold, I am laying in Zion for a foundation a Stone, a tested Stone, a precious Cornerstone of sure foundation:' He who believes - trusts in, relies on and adheres to that Stone - will not be ashamed or give way or make haste in sudden panic."*

Only as we experience Christ in these foundation truths can we become different people. The new creation message can only be experienced through the resurrected life we have in Christ Jesus.

2Timothy 2:19; *"Meanwhile, God's firm foundation is as firm as ever, these sentences engraved on the stones: GOD KNOWS WHO BELONGS TO HIM. SPURN EVIL, ALL YOU WHO NAME GOD AS GOD."* Capitals are mine

We face not only the tests of our future in this life but the judgment of God in the next life.

1Timothy 6:17-21; *"Tell those rich in this world's wealth to quit being so full of themselves and so obsessed with money, which is here today and gone tomorrow.*

Tell them to go after God, who piles on all the riches we could ever manage— to do good, to be rich in helping others, to be extravagantly generous. If they do that, they'll build a treasury that will last, gaining life that is truly life.

And oh, my dear Timothy, guard the treasure you were given! Guard it with your life. Avoid the talk-show religion and the practiced confusion of the so-called experts. People caught up in a lot of talk can miss the whole point of faith. Overwhelming grace keep you!"

Hebrews 5:12-14; *"By this time, you ought to be teachers yourselves, yet here I find you need someone to sit down with you and go over the basics on God again, starting from square one—baby's milk, when you should have been on solid food long ago! Milk is for beginners, inexperienced in God's ways; solid food is for the mature, who have some practice in telling right from wrong."*

The importance of laying the foundation is made clear as we read God's Word on this subject. The trials and tribulations will come against each believer to test his faith. It is the responsibility of each of us to ensure that our life in Christ is built on solid rock and not on shifting sand.

Matthew 7:24-27; *"These words I speak to you are not incidental additions to your life, homeowner improvements to your standard of living. They are foundational words, words to build a life on. If you work these words into your life, you are like a smart carpenter who built his house on solid rock. Rain poured down, the river flooded, a tornado hit—but nothing moved that house. It was fixed to the rock.*

But if you just use my words in Bible studies and don't work them into your life, you are like a stupid carpenter who built his house on the sandy beach. When a storm rolled in and the waves came up, it collapsed like a house of cards."

If we do not lay a proper solid foundation, then the "bricks" of knowledge along with the mortar of experience, we try to build into our life will become too heavy for the foundation to hold. Confusion and frustration and a falling away from spiritual things will result.

*'When We Have Laid A Solid Foundation,
We Can Be Confident
That Whatever We Build In God
Upon That Foundation,
Will Stand Steadfast And Sure.'

Chapter 2:

"LEARNING TO TURN AROUND."

Repentance is an about face from sin and dead works to the living God. It is an entire change of mind resulting in a total change of life. Repentance is a command of God to all.

Psalm 51; KJV. *"Have mercy upon me, O God, according to your loving kindness: according to the multitude of your tender mercies, blot out my transgressions. Wash me thoroughly from mine iniquity and cleanse me from my sin. For I acknowledge my transgressions: and my sin [is] ever before me.*

What God has already done for us has already been accomplished we need to appropriate it, and there is no better time than God's time: NOW.

Against You, and You only, have I sinned, and done [this] evil in Your sight: that You might be justified when You speak, [and] be clear when You judge. Behold, I was shaped in iniquity; and in sin did my mother conceive me. Behold, You desire truth in the inward parts: and in the hidden [part] You shall make me to know wisdom.

Clarity of relationship comes from the understanding that I, have chosen to be separated from God and therefore, it is right and proper for me to ask God to purify me, so that I may live in a righteous relationship with Him, and that can only be on His terms, not mine.

Purge me with hyssop, and I shall be clean: wash me, and I shall be whiter than snow. Make me to hear joy and gladness; [that] the bones [which] You have broken may rejoice. Hide Your face from my sins and blot out all mine iniquities. Create in me a clean heart, O God; and renew a right spirit within me. Cast me not away from Your presence; and take not Your holy spirit from me. Restore unto me the joy of Your salvation; and uphold me [with Your] free spirit.

God our heavenly Father, who is the author and finisher of my faithfulness, let me give service – be like Paul's – who because of your Grace and Mercy, gave unto him your servant, great opportunities of witness so that others may also find you their Creator in their time of need.

[Then] will I teach transgressors Your ways; and sinners shall be converted unto You. Deliver me from blood guiltiness, O God, thou God of my salvation: [and] my tongue shall sing aloud of Your righteousness. O Lord, open my lips; and my mouth shall show forth Your praise.

For You desire not sacrifice; else would I give [it]: You delight not in burnt offering. The sacrifices of God [are] a broken spirit: a broken and a contrite heart, O God, You will not despise."

It is when we are able comprehend the openness of David's heart that we can see that in this Psalm we have all the ingredients needed to approach God with such a repented heart, that God will restore us to the state in which He created us in the beginning of Genesis.

Acts 17:26-31; *"Starting from scratch, he made the entire human race and made the earth hospitable, with plenty of time and space for living so we could seek after God, and not just grope around in the dark, but actually find him. He doesn't play hide-and-seek with us. He's not remote; he's near. We live and move in him, can't get away from him!*

One of your poets said it well: 'We're the God-created.' Well, if we are the God-created, it doesn't make a lot of sense to think we could hire a sculptor to chisel a god out of stone for us, does it? "God overlooks it as long as you don't know any better—but that time is past.

Let us just for a moment reflect upon that which we know of Paul's life before and after conversion: Before conversion Paul was a strong-willed zealot of the persecution of the Christians. After conversion he was still strong-willed and still a zealot, but for Christ not against Him or the believers.

So therefore, we ask the question, what was the difference? In his B.C. life Saul appeared to be self-controlled, with his emotions on clear display. In his zealot disposition, and his religious convictions and his loyalties were Temple centered.

But in his new life – with a new name – Paul became Spirit Controlled and God centered. Not a religious fanatic but a man of Faith and Grace, just as was God's purpose for him at the very beginning of Creation.

The unknown is now known, and he's calling for a radical life-change. He has set a day when the entire human race will be judged, and everything set right. And he has already appointed the judge, confirming him before everyone by raising him from the dead."

Repentance is not optional: it is the first response we make to Christ's Lordship. He is commanding us to turn around.

Imagine a very solid steamroller at an intersection and realise that it, of itself, can do nothing. The engine needs to be turned on and the motor set into the forward or reverse gear. The brake needs to be released and then the steamroller will be engaged in a set direction either forward or reverse. Not until it has begun to move can it actually be turned away from the straight line in which it has been accustomed.

Now imagine that we are that steamroller, and the Holy Spirit is our personal driver, designated by God.

* 'The Question Is This: Have We Acknowledged His Right To Rule Over Us'?

The power of Repentance is a gift from God: He enables us to repent.

Acts 11:16-18; *"I remembered Jesus' words: 'John baptized with water; you will be baptized with the Holy Spirit.' So, I ask you: If God gave the same exact gift to*

them as to us when we believed in the Master Jesus Christ, how could I object to God? Hearing it all laid out like that, they quieted down.
And then, as it sank in, they started praising God. "It's really happened! God has broken through to the other nations, opened them up to Life!"

When God receives our confession and as an act of repentance, we suddenly realise that our actions and even our attitudes are not a private matter. We do not simply hurt ourselves and other people with our sin; we offend God. We begin to see sin as He sees it, a direct personal insult to His holiness and love.

As this truth dawns upon us - as it did David in Psalm 51; and Saul in Acts 9; - we begin to turn away from concentrating upon the things of self and to turning back to the reality of God's desire and that is to follow in His steps and in so doing we are building our relationship with Him.

It is fundamental to our relationship with God, indeed to all our earthly relationships that self is not the centre of life, but it is in the relationship we have in Him, we also in like measure have with others.

Repentance always means turning around - changing - turning from sin and our own ways to God. The common Bible words (O.T. Hebrew and N.T. Greek) bring out different emphasis; but they overlap in the basic meaning of change.

The following are from notations taken from the initial Bible School classes that I attended as a new Christian at the Moe 'New Life Christian Centre.' (1974-5)

HEBREW: The Hebrew language uses two words to describe repentance: the first emphasises emotional stirring, while the second emphasises a moral decision to forsake sin and return to God.

NAHAM: means to feel sorry, to lament, to grieve, to sigh, or to groan. The word literally refers to difficulty in breathing while one experiences intense emotion. It includes, however, the results of emotion in urging a change of behaviour and character. David did not stop with feeling bad - he turned around.

SHUWB: means to turn back, to make a radical change in attitude towards sin and God. It includes both the conscious moral separation, and a personal decision to come back to God. This word was the one most often used by the Old Testament prophets when they called God's people to turn to God once more, or return.

GREEK: The Greek language uses two complementary terms to describe genuine repentance. The first word denotes the negative aspect of repentance; the second brings out the positive change of position and relationship which results from repentance.

METANCIA: expresses the intellectual and spiritual change which occurs when a sinner turns to God. The meaning of Metancia is "to have another mind" or "to change one's mind, attitude, and purpose regarding sin." It describes an inner turning around.

EPISTREPHO: indicates the distinct change which results from repentance - a change of position in relation to God. This word can be summarised as a spiritual transition from sin to God; from death to life.

Therefore, we have defined repentance as a total change in man, and it is precisely that. Repentance changes four basic areas: emotion, will, intellect and spirit. Repentance involves the complete transfer of our love and investment; from sin and selfish aims to God.

>Matthew 22:36-40; *"Teacher, which command in God's Law is the most important?" Jesus said, 'Love the Lord your God with all your passion and prayer and intelligence.' This is the most important, the first on any list. But there is a second to set alongside it: 'Love others as well as you love yourself.' These two commands are pegs; everything in God's Law and the Prophets hangs from them."*

True repentance changes the way we feel about sin, about ourselves as sinners, and toward a holy but merciful God. True repentance includes godly sorrow for the sin we have done: a broken and contrite heart.

We experience contrition as the Holy Spirit causes us to realise the terrible affront our sin is to a holy God. He further breaks our hearts by showing us God's love and mercy even while we are in this sinful condition.

Psalm 51: 17; KJV. *"My sacrifice, the sacrifice acceptable, to God is a broken spirit; a broken and contrite heart, broken down with sorrow for sin and humbly and thoroughly penitent, such, O God, You, will not despise."*

True repentance includes deep humiliation before the Lord, in realisation of our need.

Isaiah 5: 15; Amplified: *"And the common (Metancia) man is bowed down, and the great man is brought low, and the eyes of the haughty are humbled".*

True repentance includes the sense of shame for the evil things we have done. We are ashamed of what we have made of ourselves.

Ezra 9:6; Amplified: *"Saying, O my God, I am ashamed and blush to lift my face to You, my God; for our iniquities have risen higher than our heads, and our guilt has mounted to the heavens."*

*'True Repentance Includes A Genuine Hatred Of Sin, And A Loathing Of Our Sinful Ways.'

Psalm 97:10; Amplified: *"O you, who love the Lord, hate evil; He preserves the lives of His saints, the children of God; He delivers them out of the hand of the wicked."*

Often, we find it difficult to be delivered from specific habits of sin, because we have not yet experienced sufficient hatred for sin itself, let alone the specific sin enacted.

Repentance is a complete change of mind regarding sin, a revolution of viewpoint. It includes recognition of sin for what it is.

Through repentance we are brought to the revelation – we are impacted by the knowledge – of God's evaluation of us. We surrender our broken defences against the awareness of sin and agree with God, in naming it.

> Hosea 14:1-2; Amplified: *"O Israel, return to the Lord your God, for you have stumbled and fallen, visited by calamity, due to your iniquity. Take with you, words and return unto the Lord.*
>
> *Say to Him. 'Take away all our iniquity: accept what is good and receive us graciously; so, we will render (our thanks) as bullocks (to be sacrificed) and pay the confession of our sins."*

Repentance also includes the realisation that we not only "do" sinful things, but that we are sinful people. We come to our senses and see what God has been pointing out about our need for radical change – from the inside out. We realise that God is right, and we are wrong - we are sinners!

> Psalm 51: 6; Amplified; *"Behold, You, desire truth in the inner being; make me therefore to know wisdom in my inmost heart."*

True repentance includes acknowledging God's judgment – regarding sin and our sinful condition – to be right and just.

We are able to agree with God and put away all excuse-making and self-justification.

Psalm 51:3-4; Amplified; *"For I am conscious of my transgressions, and I acknowledge them; my sin is ever before me. Against You, You, only have I sinned, and done that which is evil in Your sight; so that You are justified in Your sentence and faultless in Your judgment."*

Repentance involves the formation of a new purpose and determination. We turn away from sin and return to God.

* 'Repentance Is That Special Moment When We Make The Decision Of Our Will To Turn Around.'

First of all, we accept moral responsibility for our own actions and character. We do not put the blame for what we do and are upon others. We agree with God's judgment that we are responsible, free moral agents. Nor can we blame God for our sin.

James 1:13-15; Amplified. *"Let no one say when he is tempted, I am tempted from God; for God is incapable of being tempted by [what is] evil and He Himself tempts no one.*

An important distinction is made here between the temptations which are of the mind will and emotion – SOUL – and the testing which comes from God via the Holy Spirit – SPIRIT.

But every person is tempted when he is drawn away, enticed, and baited by his own evil desire (lust, passions).

Then the evil desire, when it has conceived, gives birth to sin, and sin, when it is fully matured, brings forth death."

Secondly, we determine to do something about our sins and the ruin of our character. We do not resign ourselves in helplessness to sin and its consequences. Instead, we like the prodigal son below, embrace the provisions of God for change through the redeeming power of the Blood of the Lamb – JESUS – the perfect sacrifice.

Luke 17-20; *"That brought him to his senses. He said, 'All those farmhands working for my father sit down to three meals a day, and here I am starving to death. I'm going back to my father. I'll say to him, Father, I've sinned against God, I've sinned before you; I don't deserve to be called your son. Take me on as a hired hand.' He got right up and went home to his father."*

Thirdly, we decide to break from sin and throw ourselves upon the mercy of God. We reject the old habits of sin to receive new life-patterns from God. As we allow God to change us in our emotion, mind, and will, by consciously co-operating with him, He changes our spiritual condition and makes us literal "new creatures."

2Corinthians 5:17-19; NKJV. *"Therefore, if anyone is in Christ, he is a new creation; old things have passed away; behold, all things have become new.*

A favourite chorus is surely:

"I'm a new creation, I'm a brand-new man,

*Old things are passed away, I'm born again.
More than a conqueror, that's who I am.
I'm a new creation, I'm a brand-new man."*

David Ingles. No 139: Praise and Worship.

Now all things are of God, who has reconciled us to Himself through Jesus Christ, and has given us the ministry of reconciliation, that is, that God was in Christ reconciling the world to Himself, not imputing their trespasses to them, and has committed to us the word of reconciliation."

* 'Repentance Is Our Response To God:
Regeneration Is God's Response To Us.'

It is a change from death to life as the Holy Spirit quickens us. The old life is, through Christ Jesus, that which Satan wants us to be constant remembrance of. However, we are assured that that old life has been taken away. Note – the debt has been paid in full, not just covered up for a future time.

Ephesians 2: 1-8; *"It wasn't so long ago that you were mired in that old stagnant life of sin. You let the world, which doesn't know the first thing about living, tell you how to live. You filled your lungs with polluted unbelief, and then exhaled disobedience.*

We all did it, all of us doing what we felt like doing, when we felt like doing it, all of us in the same boat. It's a wonder God didn't lose his temper and do away with the whole lot of us.

Instead, immense in mercy and with an incredible love, he embraced us. He took our sin-dead lives and made us alive in Christ. He did all this on his own, with no help from us! Then he picked us up and set us down in highest heaven in company with Jesus, our Messiah.
Now God has us where he wants us, with all the time in this world and the next to shower grace and kindness upon us in Christ Jesus.

Saving is all his idea, and all his work. All we do is trust him enough to let him do it. It's God's gift from start to finish!"

* 'This New Life Is The Change From The Kingdom Of Darkness To God's Kingdom Of Light.'

Remember the story of the Prodigal Son mentioned earlier; It is an illustration of the change from alienation to acceptance.

Ephesians 2:11-18; *"But don't take any of this for granted. It was only yesterday that you outsiders to God's ways had no idea of any of this, didn't know the first thing about the way God works, hadn't the faintest idea of Christ. You knew nothing of that rich history of God's covenants and promises in Israel, hadn't a clue about what God was doing in the world at large.*

Now because of Christ—dying that death, shedding that blood—you who were once out of it altogether are in on everything. The Messiah has made things up between us so that we're now together on this. Both non-Jewish outsiders and Jewish insiders. He tore down the wall we used to keep each other at a distance.

He repealed the law code that had become so clogged with fine print and footnotes that it hindered more than it helped. Then he started over. Instead of continuing with two groups of people separated by centuries of animosity and suspicion, he created a new kind of human being, a fresh start for everybody.

Christ brought us together through his death on the Cross. The Cross got us to embrace, and that was the end of the hostility. Christ came and preached peace to you outsiders and peace to us insiders. He treated us as equals, and so made us equals. Through him we both share the same Spirit and have equal access to the Father."

Yet another chorus that I have embraced and love to sing is:

> We are heirs of the Father,
> We are joint heirs with the Son.
> We are children of the Kingdom.
> We are family, we are one.
> Authored by J. & C. Owen. No. 281 Praise & Worship.

Chapter 3.

"WHAT IS THE BASIS FOR REPENTANCE?"

Another chorus which has been a constant joy to sing is:

'He brought me out of the kingdom of darkness, and into His glorious light.
I'm on the rock of salvation and I fear night day or night.
I have the peace down in my soul, and oh! how the glories roll. I'm free, I'm free, I'm free, praise God I'm free!'
The author must be God via the Holy Spirit. No.53 Praise & Worship.

1John 1:5-10; KJV.[1] *"This then, is the message which we have heard of him, and declare to you, that God is light, and in him is no darkness at all.*

If we say that we have fellowship with him, and walk in darkness, we lie, and do not the truth: But if we walk in the light, as he is in the light, we have fellowship one with another, and the blood of Jesus Christ his Son cleanses us from all sin.

If we say that we have no sin, we deceive ourselves, and the truth is not in us. If we confess our sins, he is faithful and just to forgive us [our] sins, and to cleanse us from all unrighteousness.

If we say that we have not sinned, we make him a liar, and his word is not in us.

Sin breaks all relationship with God - and continues to do so each and every time we give in to sin. We must realize the seriousness and gravity of sin because it cost the shedding of blood. God's purpose for man can only be fully realized by man's reconciliation to God. Man was created for the pleasure of God, but both his fellowship with God and his ability to serve God were lost through sin. This involves restoration in spirit, soul, and body. This restoration - often called "salvation" - brings life.

Ezekiel 18: 23, 28; Amplified: *"Have I any pleasure in the death of the wicked? Says the Lord, and not rather that he should turn from his evil way and return to his God and live ... Because he considers and turns away from all his transgressions which he has committed, he shall surely live; he shall not die."*

Man, in his sinful condition, cannot approach God directly and be accepted. Before God can look upon man, the sin question must be solved. An old chorus I love to sing, and I am always in remembrance of the words:

*'I am covered over with the robe of righteousness,
that Jesus gives to me, gives to me.
I am covered over with the precious blood of Jesus,
and He lives in me, lives in me. What a joy it is to know
my heavenly father loves me so and gives to me, my Jesus.
When He looks at me, He sees not what I used to be, but He
sees Jesus.'* Author is unknown. Resource Chorus Book No. 235.

God has done this by means of substitutionary and vicarious sacrifice – which simply means – the Replacement, *and in the part of one subject matter, for another.*

During the Old Testament times, the blood of sacrificial animals was accepted as a covering for sin. But this had only a temporary effectiveness. Not until Jesus Christ became the Lamb of God to die in our place, was sin completely removed and sent away. His blood was perfect:

His sacrifice of Himself was accepted as the complete ransom / redemption by God. Christ as that Sacrificial Lamb became the complete and full payment for all sin: Forever.

2Corinthians 5:17-20; NKJV. *"Therefore, if anyone is in Christ, he is a new creation; old things have passed away; behold, all things have become new.*

Now all things are of God, who has reconciled us to Himself through Jesus Christ, and has given us the ministry of reconciliation, that is, that God was in Christ reconciling the world to Himself, not imputing their trespasses to them, and has committed to us the word of reconciliation.

Now then, we are ambassadors for Christ, as though God were pleading through us: we implore you on Christ's behalf, be reconciled to God."

Sin has totally ruined man's capacity to please God. The Bible describes man's ruin as corruption and spiritual death. Theologians sometimes speak of the destruction of man's capacity for God through sin as: "Total Depravity".

By this they mean that man is not only lost, but unable to help himself. God knew that He alone could and indeed must take the initiative in saving mankind from himself.

Job 15: 14-16; Amplified: *"What is man, that he can be pure and clean? And he that is born of a woman, that he can be right and just?*

Behold God puts no trust in His holy ones, the angels; indeed, the heavens are not clean in His sight. How much less that which is abominable and corrupt, a man who drinks iniquity like water?"

Basic to all sin is selfishness as opposed to godliness. Sin is loving ourselves and preferring our own ways, instead of loving God and seeking to please Him.

Romans 3:9-12; *"So where does that put us? Do we Jews get a better break than the others? Not really. Basically, all of us, whether insiders or outsiders, start out in identical conditions, which is to say that we all start out as sinners.*

Scripture leaves no doubt about it: There's nobody living right, not even one, nobody who knows the score, nobody alert for God. They've all taken the wrong turn; they've all wandered down blind alleys. No one's living right; I can't find a single one."

It is a vital that we understand that sin can be either that of commission - doing anything which is not God's will for us, or that of omission - failing to do what is God's will.

It is in fact, making decisions to rebel instead of to obey. Sin is our own choice of will as against God's will; the use of our capacity to decide – ME OR GOD!!

Isaiah 53:6; Amplified: *"All we like sheep have gone astray, we have turned everyone to his own way; and the Lord has made to light on Him the guilt and iniquity of us all."*

Both the Hebrew and the Greek languages use several words to describe the condition and expression of man's basic selfishness and rebellion against God. Among the more common words for sin in the New Testament are the following:

HAMARTIA *(ha-mar-ti-a)*. This word summarizes sin as our failure to be the person God intended us to be. The dictionary definition is "to miss the mark; to be in error; to fall short.

"We have missed the target of fulfilling God's glorious plans for us."

Romans 3:21-26; *"But in our time, something new has been added. What Moses and the prophets witnessed to all those years has happened. The God-setting-things-right that we read about has become Jesus-setting-things-right for us.*

And not only for us, but for everyone who believes in him. For there is no difference between us and them in this. Since we've compiled this long and sorry record as sinners (both us and them) and proved that we are utterly incapable of living the glorious lives God wills for us, God did it for us.

Out of sheer generosity he put us in right standing with himself. A pure gift. He got us out of the mess we're in and restored us to where he always wanted us to be. And he did it by means of Jesus Christ.

God sacrificed Jesus on the altar of the world to clear that world of sin. Having faith in him sets us in the clear. God decided on this course of action in full view of the public—to set the world in the clear with himself through the sacrifice of Jesus, finally taking care of the sins, he had so patiently endured.

This is not only clear, but it's now—this is current history! God sets things right. He also makes it possible for us to live in his rightness."

Hamartia describes sin in a three-fold way: The source of wrong actions. It is a power which acts through the members of our physical bodies, thus wrong actions created by our wrong thinking. W.E. Vine states that 'Sin as an organized power, acting through the members of the body, though the seat of sin is in the will – the body is the organic instrument;'

In a book – still in its embryonic stage – I will deal more comprehensively upon this subject concerning the personal desire to escape from wrong actions. Its title says it all "Getting Rid of Stinking Thinking." Scheduled to be released by the end of 2024/25

We must understand that 'Sin' is, at its root 'moral wickedness.' Sin is more than doing the wrong thing. Mistakes are doing the wrong thing but without the wrong motives, therefore mistakes are not necessarily sin.

* 'It Is From Within, That Sin Arises,
And That Is So, Because Of Man's Basic Corruption.'

Sin involves the corruption of a person's character because it emphasizes moral badness or evil, so to speak, within that person. This position, clearly indicated by Jesus, is found in the Gospel of Mark:

Mark 7:14-23; *"Jesus called the crowd together again and said, "Listen now, all of you—take this to heart. It's not what you swallow that pollutes your life; it's what you vomit—that's the real pollution."*

When he was back home after being with the crowd, his disciples said, "We don't get it. Put it in plain language." Jesus said, "Are you being wilfully stupid? Don't you see that what you swallow can't contaminate you?

It doesn't enter your heart but your stomach, works its way through the intestines, and is finally flushed." (That took care of dietary quibbling; Jesus was saying that all foods are fit to eat.)

Sin is not physical but spiritual, it attacks through our soul – thus through our Mind, Will and Emotions – each of which we have in Christ Jesus the power to control.

He went on: "It's what comes out of a person that pollutes: obscenities, lusts, thefts, murders, adulteries, greed, depravity, deceptive dealings, carousing, mean looks, slander, arrogance, foolishness— all these are vomit from the heart. There is the source of your pollution."

Sin is wilful transgression of the law – it is the violation of God's law, deliberately stepping across the border between right and wrong, so to speak. Therefore, such action – stepping across – is not accidental or without knowledge of an objective moral law, it is stepping out from within the safe barriers of Law into a lawlessness which does not impute Godly values but instead places us outside of our righteous relationship, both with God and our fellow mankind.

* 'Transgression Is Man's Invasion Of Forbidden Territory Or Crossing Over The Moral Boundaries God Has Established.'

Romans 4:15-16; *"A contract drawn up by a hard-nosed lawyer and with plenty of fine print only makes sure that you will never be able to collect. But if there is no contract in the first place, simply a promise—and God's promise at that—you can't break it.*

This is why the fulfillment of God's promise depends entirely on trusting God and his way, and then simply embracing him and what he does. God's promise arrives as pure gift. That's the only way everyone can be sure to get in on it, those who keep the religious traditions and those who have never heard of them. For Abraham is father of us all. He is not our racial father—that's reading the story backwards. He is our faith father."

Lawlessness is the irritation of our times. Sin not only includes the indwelling source of sin and its many manifestations, but the guiding principle of life. Lawlessness is a lifestyle of refusing to be subject to God's law. This is more than disobedience; it is total disregard for the existence of the law.

Romans 2:12-16; *"If you sin without knowing what you're doing, God takes that into account. But if you sin knowing full well what you're doing, that's a different story entirely. Merely hearing God's law is a waste of your time if you don't do what he commands. Doing, not hearing, is what makes the difference with God.*

When outsiders who have never heard of God's law follow it more or less by instinct, they confirm its truth by their obedience.

They show that God's law is not something alien, imposed on us from without, but woven into the very fabric of our creation. There is something deep within them that echoes God's yes and no, right, and wrong.

Their response to God's yes and no will become public knowledge on the day God makes his final decision about every man and woman. The Message from God that I proclaim through Jesus Christ takes into account all these differences."

    * 'The Most Important Result Of Sin Is That It
       Breaks The Fellowship Both With God,
  And Our Fellowship With All That He Created.'

It also does things to our own personal inner workings. When we say that the wage of sin is death, this does not simply speak of the final accounting at the end of life, because Sin produces results from the very moment of action. It is always to be seen in the present tense because the effects will permeate from the very beginning and last into the future.

The death process is set in motion the moment we sin, and it cuts off the flow of God's life, within us. This is why immediate repentance is so necessary. Sin must be washed out of us before it destroys us from within.

    1John 3:18-24; "*My dear children, let's not just talk about love; let's practice real love. This is the only way we'll know we're living truly, living in God's reality. It's also the way to shut down debilitating self-criticism, even when there is something to it. For God is greater than our worried hearts and knows more about us than we do ourselves.*

As I discovered this revelationary Scripture, it allowed me to experience a new and invigorating lifestyle enabling me to have a positive goal to work towards thus allowing that Anticipated Expectation of my future to breath new air, so to speak.

And friends, once that's taken care of and we're no longer accusing or condemning ourselves, we're bold and free before God! We're able to stretch our hands out and receive what we asked for because we're doing what he said, doing what pleases him.

Again, this is God's command: to believe in his personally named Son, Jesus Christ. He told us to love each other, in line with the original command.

As we keep his commands, we live deeply and surely in him, and he lives in us. And this is how we experience his deep and abiding presence in us: by the Spirit, he gave us."

Sin makes us less of a person. Each time we sin, we become less the person we were intended to be. Something dies within us.

We know something about ourselves that makes us think less of ourselves. Self-esteem is lowered. If we cannot respect ourselves, it is hard for us to expect others to respect us. We lose confidence both before other people and especially before God.

Visualise a traffic light.

AMBER: WE CALL IT "CONSCIENCE." Sin creates guilt and that is why God has built into us an inner alarm system to tell us the difference between right and wrong.

RED: WE CALL IT "GUILT." It is possible to alter the conscience until it is no longer accurate, but its purpose is to give us basic moral guidance. When the alarm is sounding, telling us something is wrong: This feeling of inner conviction demands attention. We must deal with it in some way and of course this means STOP WHAT WE ARE DOING.

The two ways we can respond to guilt are: AMBER; confessing the sin and receiving forgiveness, or RED by seeking punishment - even if we have to punish ourselves.

GREEN: We call it 'Living in Faith:' *my first book.*

God's answer to guilt is the way of repentance: confess, ask for forgiveness, receive His cleansing and then walking towards Him and therefore away from the sin. This is the ROCK and the PATHWAY upon which our life's journey becomes alive and the promises He has given us are fulfilled.

>1John 1:1-10; *"From the very first day, we were there, taking it all in—we heard it with our own ears, saw it with our own eyes, verified it with our own hands. The Word of Life appeared right before our eyes; we saw it happen! And now we're telling you in most sober prose that what we witnessed was, incredibly, this: The infinite Life of God himself took shape before us.*

I had over the course of my first 37 years of life, had a very rough time, and I tried many times to understand this 'God Thing.' I attended church spasmodically over the youth and early adult years, but no one ever talked about the Holy Spirit and as a result there were no manifestations of His power either.

From a very personal perspective I know that I would not be here enjoying my life in Jesus if it had not been for the demonstrations of Jesus and the Holy Spirit which were not in evidence in those early years before my Christian walk began. But when I entered that first Pentecostal assembly I heard and saw the Power of God and the unconditional Love which I felt was just so, so powerful.

And I can testify that I have never turned away from that irrefutable evidence, which was manifested before my eyes, because I 'knew' because I 'saw,' and I heard, and it was explained to me, as a witness of God's supreme power. This is what has compelled me from that evening and the forty-seven years and counting, until now to tell – to witness – all that I have seen and heard concerning Jesus and the plan and purposes of God, Who is my Creator, in the Faith, which is better known as Christianity.

We saw it, we heard it, and now we're telling you so you can experience it along with us, this experience of communion with the Father and his Son, Jesus Christ. Our motive for writing is simply this: We want you to enjoy this, too. Your joy will double our joy!

This is surely the cause and effect of living in Faith and witnessing that others might be saved from sin not by man but by the power of God and the gift of His Grace poured out for us through the death and the resurrection of Jesus.

This, in essence, is the message we heard from Christ and are passing on to you: God is light, pure light; there's not a trace of darkness in him. If we claim that we experience a shared life with him and continue to stumble around in the dark, we're obviously lying through our teeth—we're not living what we claim."
But if we walk in the light, God himself being the light, we also experience a shared life with one another, as the sacrificed blood of Jesus, God's Son, purges all our sin.

Another truth that is fundamental in our Christian walk is that 'By our fruits we shall be known.' If this is to be an effective gauge, we must be able to see both in our own lives and within the lives of those around us, the real fruit of our testimony – or theirs - whether it be good fruit or bad.

If we claim that we're free of sin, we're only fooling ourselves. A claim like that is errant nonsense. On the other hand, if we admit our sins—make a clean breast of them—he won't let us down; he'll be true to himself. He'll forgive our sins and purge us of all wrongdoing If we claim that we've never sinned, we out-and-out contradict God—make a liar out of him. A claim like that only shows off our ignorance of God."

So, therefore it is important that we press the point that 'walking in the light' is the only way that we can have security in His Promises.

'Walking in the Light' was my first series of Bible Study Material in Western Australia 1981 – 1990 – for the new believers whom God had inspired Noelene and I to bring into congregations in communities across that State. *The contents of this set of study material are contained in my fourth book 'A New Way of Living'.*

Paul talks about a continuance in God's presence. God is light. If we remain in fellowship with him, He exposes us to ourselves little by little, as we can bear it. He brings to the surface things that need to be changed in us.

Of two thing we can be absolutely sure:

1: Gods Word Will Always Bring Light And Life, To Those Who Believe In Him.
2: Satan Will Always Bring Darkness And Death, Because Our Sin, Has A Will Of Its Own Kind, Separate Us From God.

Each sinful act makes it easier for us to do the same thing again. And the only way out is through personal confession and repentance, overcoming the habits of sin and therefore enabling us to renounce them. When we renounce something, we are determined in our hearts to be finished with it.

To be finished with it must entail that we have an alternative course of action and that is to turn towards God Who has given us a better way, truth, and life, to live.

2 Corinthians 4:1-4; *"Since God has so generously let us in on what he is doing, we're not about to throw up our hands and walk off the job just because we run into occasional hard times.*

We refuse to wear masks- concealing our real identity* *– and play games. We don't manoeuvre and manipulate behind the scenes. And we don't twist God's Word to suit ourselves. Rather, we keep everything we do and say out in the open, the whole truth on display, so that those who want to can see and judge for themselves in the presence of God.*

If our Message is obscure to anyone, it's not because we're holding back in any way. No, it's because these other people are looking or going the wrong way and refuse to give it serious attention.

All they have eyes for is the fashionable god of darkness. They think he can give them what they want, and that they won't have to bother believing a Truth they can't see. They're stone-blind to the dayspring brightness of the Message that shines with Christ, who gives us the best picture of God we'll ever get."

*In the above passage I have imposed an explanation in small print, so that in this present age of Covid restrictions 2022 in Australia, we do not confuse the current law re masks with the concept revealed in the Scripture. P.B.

If we co-operate with the Holy Spirit as He shows us what we look like to God, we not only continue to enjoy a blessed relationship with Him, but we experience constant cleansing and growth. This is really another way to describe a life of continual repentance.

Several congregations of believers in Sri Lanka now boldly display this verse from the Psalm of David:

> Psalm 119:105; KJV. *'Lord, your word is a lamp for my feet and a light for my pathway'.*

This is also the standard Scripture of the ministry of Acts 29ers International which God has allowed me to lead for the past 19 years in that country. P.B.

Perhaps I can pass on to you a piece of advice given to me by my pastor and mentor the late Pastor Lyall Potts of the Moe New Life Centre C.R.C., some 47 years ago:

* "The Bible is meant to be a personal letter from the heart of the Father (GOD) to the heart of the child of God (ME). And when I respond; it is from the heart of the child (ME) to the heart of my Father (GOD)." So, this is how I receive the advice:

> Psalm 119 v105: PBR-H *"Father, your word is like a lamp to show me where I stand today, at this moment of my life. Your lamp shows me and encourages me in the*

knowledge that I stand on solid ground and rooted in the Rock of my Salvation, Jesus my Saviour, and Lord.

Father, I thank you also for the light of your word which gives me confidence to walk with certainty along the pathway of life which I now live, in you," AMEN.

Salvation is not a once-in-a-lifetime experience. It does not consist of initial repentance alone. There is no such statement in God's word which tells us that once I have said 'yes' to Jesus and entered into a Salvation relationship with him that I will always be saved.

Because to have that 'got-you' moment would be an abuse of God's promise of choice, in other words He would have deprived us of our free will.

I have never doubted God's promise to me that He would never leave nor stop loving me. But that is God's promise to me, that is God's commitment to me, and I believe He will be able to maintain that promise for eternity.

However, my promise to Him is of my personal persuasion. My personal decision to follow, is dependent upon my resolve to build my relationship with Him as my Father, my Guide and Mentor, and my deliverer from darkness. It never can be that making a once in a lifetime commitment absolves me from ever falling into sin.

I can confess that since I was "saved" at the Moe New Life Centre and confessed not only my sins already committed but my decision to turn away, repent, that style of living and to follow in His footsteps, I have sadly fallen short many times, as have all who read these words – because all have fallen short of the mark of salvation, have we not?

Many of us do not understand that salvation does not only have a past meaning, the forgiveness of our sin, but present and future application in being made like Christ. The truth of the matter is simply put;

> * 'We Must Lay The Foundation Stone Of Initial Repentance,
> In Order To Go On Changing, The Rest Of Our Lives.'

Note that the word – changing – implies us to a continuous life of change. To go on changing requires the on-going repentance and acknowledging of our constant need of the Lord in practical daily needs.

We have been confused about the nature of sin and of repentance, and this confusion hinders us from simply accepting God's light and cleansing on an up-to-date basis.

Temptation is not a sin. Jesus was sinless; however, He experienced every kind of temptation. He was directly assaulted by Satan in the wilderness with a flood of temptations aimed at His most vulnerable moments.

> Luke 4:1-13; *"Now Jesus, full of the Holy Spirit, left the Jordan and was led by the Spirit into the wild. For forty wilderness days and nights he was tested by the Devil. He ate nothing during those days, and when the time was up, he was hungry.*

This testing was a time when Satan observed Jesus's strengths and weaknesses. We can find many times when God is testing us, both from within the Scriptures and also the ways in which we life out what we believe. However, it is always Satan who tempts us. We see in this passage the glaring temptations which Satan employs to break our spirit – our relationship with God – put into practice. We also see that Jesus used the Word of His Father – God – to overcome such temptations and thereby showing us of this and all generations how to effectively overcome Satan and his lies.

The Devil, playing on his hunger, gave the first test: 'Since you're God's Son, command this stone to turn into a loaf of bread'. Jesus answered by quoting Deuteronomy: 'It takes more than bread to really live.'

For the second test he led him up and spread out all the kingdoms of the earth on display at once. Then the Devil said, 'They're yours in their entire splendor to serve your pleasure. I'm in charge of them all and can turn them over to whomever I wish. Worship me and they're yours, the whole works.' Jesus refused, again backing his refusal with Deuteronomy: 'Worship the Lord your God and only the Lord your God. Serve him with absolute single heartedness.'

For the third test the Devil took him to Jerusalem and put him on top of the Temple. He said, 'If you are God's Son, jump. It's written, isn't it, that he has placed you in the care of angels to protect you; they will catch you; you won't so much as stub your toe on a stone'?

'Yes,' said Jesus, 'and it's also written, don't you dare tempt the Lord your God.' That completed the testing. The Devil retreated temporarily, lying in wait for another opportunity."

Temptation is a strong pull or push to sin. As we have already said,

* 'Temptation Is Not Sin Itself, Unless We Give In To It.'

As the song puts it, *"Yielding is sin."* It is not the feeling of temptation but the decision of our will that results in sinful action. Because more often than not we confuse condemnation for the reproof of the Spirit, and therefore enter into the darkness which will then bring self-shame upon us.

The Holy Spirit's reproof comes as truth and as light. It makes manifest both the problem and the solution. It is specific. God, in and through His Word does not reprove but reproofs us, fortifying our relationship potential In Him.

2 Timothy 3:16-17; *"Every part of Scripture is God-breathed and useful one way or another—showing us truth, exposing our rebellion, correcting our mistakes, training us to live God's way. Through the Word we are put together and shaped up for the tasks God has for us."*

Condemnation brings cloudiness and a vague self-hatred. It tells us we are all wrong but does not provide constructive criticism. God's reproof is uplifting and helpful; condemnation seeks to tear us down and to create general discouragement.

The Bible tells us that God never uses condemnation in dealing with us; we do not have to put up with its bullying thoughts and feelings.

When the Holy Spirit deals with us, even about sin and faults, He does it according to the law of the Spirit of life in Christ Jesus.

Romans 8:1-2; KJV. *"Therefore, there is now no condemnation of those who are in the Christ Jesus, who walk not after the flesh but after the Spirit."*

We try to; "earn" our forgiveness, when in fact the price for forgiveness has already been paid in full, by Christ.

All we need to do is to receive it, and to then realize and acknowledge our need for it, and to ask for it continually. Asking opens us to receive from God. The Bible does not teach that we need to have any kind of punishment inflicted upon us to make us feel sorry. As we have read earlier in this chapter the Holy Spirit gives repentance, which includes both sorrow for sin and the ability to turn away from it.

Acts 5:27-32; *"Bringing them back, they stood them before the High Council. The Chief Priest said, "Didn't we give you strict orders not to teach in Jesus' name? And here you have filled Jerusalem with your teaching and are trying your best to blame us for the death of this man."*

Peter and the apostles answered, "It's necessary to obey God rather than men. The God of our ancestors raised up Jesus, the One you killed by hanging him on a cross. God set him on high at his side, Prince, and Saviour, to give Israel the gift of a changed life and sins forgiven.

And we are witnesses to these things. The Holy Spirit, whom God gives to those who obey him, corroborates every detail."

The apostles and believers were noticeably confident of the promises of God and thus were never fearful of man's law representative in their day, as the Laws of Moses or indeed the Roman Law, present in their country, at that time.

Galatians 5:17-21; *"For there is a root of sinful self-interest in us that is at odds with a free spirit, just as the free spirit is incompatible with selfishness. These two ways of life are antithetical, so that you cannot live at times one way and at times another way according to how you feel on any given day. Why don't you choose to be led by the Spirit and so escape the erratic compulsions of a law-dominated existence?"*

This must also be for us, the time when we stand confident of the power of Godly witness in the lives of believers, in this era, some 2000 years A.D.

There is this constant move within societies worldwide, to move away from Godly principles and to enact laws that are divisive, particularly concerning those things which are seen as 'Christian Values.'

It is those same values which have brought us out of the 'dark ages' that are now under threat. The Christian standards are being shunted and the Humanistic Values – such as they are – are gaining an ascendancy which bodes a Godless society and a silent Christian Church.

Rather than our silent – if not acquiescent – approach, it is surely the challenge to this current generation of believers in Jesus, to stand up to the bullying tactics of those who would breakdown Christian values, and to express those same values and integrity – the very principals of Christian life and the living of it, just as did the apostles and disciples or the early Christian Church.

CHAPTER 4.

"PREPARE THE WAY OF THE LORD:"

We cannot begin 'a new life' in Christ without first turning totally away from our old life of sin. Repentance is the inner transition from self-dependence and self-government – to an absolute submission to God. Kingdom means having someone rule over us – having a real king.

Two Old Testament passages gives us an insight into the way that our God desires for us to go:

Isaiah 40:1-5; KJV. *"Comfort you, comfort you my people, says your God. Speak you comfortably to Jerusalem, and cry to her, that her warfare is accomplished, that her iniquity is pardoned: for she has received of the LORD'S hand double for all her sins.*

The voice of him that cries in the wilderness, Prepare you the way of the LORD, make straight in the desert a highway for our God. Every valley shall be exalted, and every mountain and hill shall be made low: and the crooked shall be made straight, and the rough places plain: And the glory of the LORD shall be revealed, and all flesh shall see [it] together: for the mouth of the LORD has spoken [it]."

Jeremiah 4:1-4; KJV. *"If you would return, O Israel, says the LORD, return to me: and if you will put away your abominations out of my sight, then shall you not remove. And you shall swear, The LORD lives, in truth, in judgment, and in righteousness; and the nations shall bless themselves in Him, and in Him shall they glory.*

For thus says the LORD to the men of Judah and Jerusalem, Break up your fallow ground, and sow not among thorns. Circumcise yourselves to the LORD, and take away the foreskins of your heart, you men of Judah and inhabitants of Jerusalem: lest my fury come forth like fire, and burn that none can quench [it], because of the evil of your doings."

We cannot crown Jesus Lord of our lives in practical experience except through the assistance of the Holy Spirit in the realm of repentance.

Calling Jesus, "Lord" with full biblical meaning requires the renouncing of 'self'-rule or imagined "independence". It includes the acknowledgment of the need of someone else to guide and direct our lives. Repentance is our acknowledgment that we are finished with the way we have been living and are ready to embrace His new life.

This transference of dependence was considered so basic in the New Testament that every major teacher introduced the gospel with the necessity of repentance. The following are just some of those examples:

John the Baptist:
    Matthew 3:1-3; Amplified. *"IN THOSE days there appeared John the Baptist, preaching in the Wilderness (Desert) of Judea And saying, Repent (think differently;*

change your mind, regretting your sins and changing your conduct), for the kingdom of heaven is at hand.

This is he who was mentioned by the prophet Isaiah when he said, The voice of one crying in the wilderness (shouting in the desert), Prepare the road for the Lord, make His highways straight (level, direct)."

Jesus Himself:

Matthew 4:17; Amplified. *"From that time Jesus began to preach, crying out, Repent (change your mind for the better, heartily amend your ways, with abhorrence of your past sins), for the kingdom of heaven is at hand.*

The Twelve Disciples:

Mark 6:12; Amplified. *"So, they went out and preached that men should repent [that they should change their minds for the better and heartily amend their ways, with abhorrence of their past sins]."*

The Apostle Paul:

Acts 26:13-20; Amplified. *"When on the road at midday, O king, I saw a light from heaven surpassing the brightness of the sun, flashing about me and those who were traveling with me.*

And when we had all fallen to the ground, I heard a voice in the Hebrew tongue saying to me, Saul, Saul, why do you continue to persecute Me [to harass and trouble and molest Me]? It is dangerous and turns out badly for you to keep kicking against the goads [to keep offering vain and perilous resistance]. And I said, Who are You, Lord?

And the Lord said, I am Jesus, Whom you are persecuting. But arise and stand upon your feet; for I have appeared to you for this purpose, that I might appoint you to serve as [My] minister and to bear witness both to what you have seen of Me and to that in which I will appear to you,

Mankind may consider themselves to be God's messengers but in reality, the anointing of ministry is the sovereign responsibility of God. The assuredness of this is comfort to the believer because God does not make bad decisions, EVER. But we can and do make bad decisions, more often than any of us choose to admit.

Choosing you out [selecting you for Myself] and delivering you from among this [Jewish] people and the Gentiles to whom I am sending you— To open their eyes that they may turn from darkness to light, and from the power of Satan to God, so that they may thus receive forgiveness and release from their sins and a place and portion among those who are consecrated and purified by faith in Me.

Wherefore, O King Agrippa, I was not disobedient unto the heavenly vision but made known openly first of all to those at Damascus, then at Jerusalem and throughout the whole land of Judea, and also among the Gentiles, that they should repent and turn to God, and do works and live lives consistent with and worthy of their repentance."

The Apostle Peter:

Acts 2:36-39; *"All Israel, then, know this: There's no longer room for doubt—God made him Master and Messiah, this Jesus whom you killed on a cross."*

Cut to the quick, those who were there listening asked Peter and the other apostles, "Brothers! Brothers! So now what do we do?"

Peter said, "Change your life. Turn to God and be baptized, each of you, in the name of Jesus Christ, so your sins are forgiven. Receive the gift of the Holy Spirit. The promise is targeted to you and your children, but also to all who are far away—whomever, in fact, our Master God invites."

Laying the foundation of repentance from dead works includes first of all the initial repentance, which turns us from darkness to light. We see ourselves as sinners in God's sight and acknowledge this. We turn from our life of sin to God. But repentance does not end there; this is only the beginning.

Initial repentance is like a door into a whole new world of a continuing repentance. As we come to know God's love and holiness more and more, we see ourselves in increasing need of change in three areas:

* 'Acknowledgment Of Our Need For Change, Sorrow For Being Unlike God In Character, Continuing In Repentance.'

The Lord Jesus continues to examine us for evidence of repentance as He walks among His people today. We notice, for example, in the book of Revelation, Jesus is walking in the midst of the seven local churches. To five out of the seven, He warns them that He must see repentance on their part, or they will experience severe loss.

The difference between initial repentance and continuing repentance is this: Initially we repent for what we are - sinners; then after this confession of who we are, we repent for what we do or fail to do – that is those specific sins we can remember we have done, or indeed are continuing to do.

God's messages to those five Churches are summed up in the following passages;

1. Ephesus:

Revelation 2:1-7; *"Write this to Ephesus, to the Angel of the church. The One with Seven Stars in his right-fist grip, striding through the golden seven-lights' circle, speaks:*

"I see what you've done, your hard, hard work, your refusal to quit. I know you can't stomach evil, that you weed out apostolic pretenders. I know your persistence, your courage in my cause, that you never wear out.

"But you walked away from your first love—why? What's going on with you, anyway? Do you have any idea how far

you've fallen? A Lucifer fall! Turn back! Recover your dear early love. No time to waste, for I'm well on my way to removing your light from the golden circle.
"You do have this to your credit: You hate the Nicolaitan business. I hate it, too.

Are your ears awake? Listen. Listen to the Wind Words, the Spirit blowing through the churches. I'm about to call each conqueror to dinner. I'm spreading a banquet of Tree-of-Life fruit, a supper plucked from God's orchard."

2. Pergamos:

Revelation 2:12-17; "*Write this to Pergamum, to the Angel of the church. The One with the sharp-biting sword draws from the sheath of his mouth—out come the sword words:*

I see where you live, right under the shadow of Satan's throne. But you continue boldly in my Name; you never once denied my Name, even when the pressure was worst, when they martyred Antipas, my witness who stayed faithful to me on Satan's turf.

But why do you indulge that Balaam crowd? Don't you remember that Balaam was an enemy agent, seducing Balak and sabotaging Israel's holy pilgrimage by throwing unholy parties? And why do you put up with the Nicolaitans, who do the same thing?

Enough! Don't give in to them; I'll be with you soon. I'm fed up and about to cut them to pieces with my sword-sharp words.

Are your ears awake? Listen. Listen to the Wind Words, the Spirit blowing through the churches.
I'll give the sacred manna to every conqueror; I'll also give a clear, smooth stone inscribed with your new name, your secret new name."

3.   Thyatira:

Revelation 2:18-29; *"Write this to Thyatira, to the Angel of the church. God's Son, eyes pouring fire-blaze, standing on feet of furnace-fired bronze, says this:*

I see everything you're doing for me. Impressive! The love and the faith, the service and persistence. Yes, very impressive! You get better at it every day.

But why do you let that Jezebel who calls herself a prophet mislead my dear servants into Cross-denying, self-indulging religion? I gave her a chance to change her ways, but she has no intention of giving up a career in the god-business. I'm about to lay her low, along with her partners, as they play their sex-and-religion games.

The bastard offspring of their idol-whoring I'll kill. Then every church will know that appearances don't impress me. I x-ray every motive and make sure you get what's coming to you.

The rest of you Thyatirids, who have nothing to do with this outrage, who scorn this playing around with the Devil that gets paraded as profundity, be assured I'll not make life any harder for you than it already is. Hold on to the truth you have until I get there.

Here's the reward I have for every conqueror, everyone who keeps at it, refusing to give up: You'll rule the nations, your Shepherd-King rule as firm as an iron staff, their resistance fragile as clay pots. This was the gift my Father gave me; I pass it along to you — and with it, the Morning Star! Are your ears awake? Listen. Listen to the Wind Words, the Spirit blowing through the churches."

4. Sardis:

Revelation 3:1-6; "*Write this to Sardis, to the Angel of the church. The One holding the Seven Spirits of God in one hand, a firm grip on the Seven Stars with the other, speaks:* "*I see right through your work. You have a reputation for vigour and zest, but you're dead, stone dead.*

"*Up on your feet! Take a deep breath! Maybe there's life in you yet. But I wouldn't know it by looking at your busywork; nothing of God's work has been completed. Your condition is desperate.*

Think of the gift you once had in your hands, the Message you heard with your ears—grasp it again and turn back to God. "*If you pull the covers back over your head and sleep on, oblivious to God, I'll return when you least expect it, break into your life like a thief in the night.*

You still have a few Christians in Sardis who haven't ruined themselves wallowing in the muck of the world's ways. They'll walk with me on parade! They've proved their worth! Conquerors will march in the victory parade, their names indelible in the Book of Life. I'll lead them up and present them by name to my Father and his Angels.

Are your ears awake? Listen. Listen to the Wind Words, the Spirit blowing through the churches."

5. Laodicea:

Revelation 3:14-22; *"Write to Laodicea, to the Angel of the church. God's Yes, the Faithful and Accurate Witness, the First of God's creation, says:*

I know you inside and out and find little to my liking. You're not cold, you're not hot—far better to be either cold or hot! You're stale. You're stagnant. You make me want to vomit.
You brag, 'I'm rich, I've got it made, I need nothing from anyone,' oblivious that in fact you're a pitiful, blind beggar, threadbare and homeless.

Here's what I want you to do: Buy your gold from me, gold that's been through the refiner's fire. Then you'll be rich. Buy your clothes from me, clothes designed in Heaven. You've gone around half-naked long enough. And buy medicine for your eyes from me so you can see, really see.

The people I love, I call to account—prod and correct and guide so that they'll live at their best. Up on your feet, then!

About face! Run after God! Look at me. I stand at the door. I knock. If you hear me call and open the door, I'll come right in and sit down to supper with you.

Conquerors will sit alongside me at the head table, just as I, having conquered, took the place of honour at the side of my Father. That's my gift to the conquerors! Are your ears awake? Listen. Listen to the Wind Words, the Spirit blowing through the churches."

Yes, it is so very, very true, that just as in the churches of this the 21st century A.D. so also, every one of those churches mentioned in the book of 'Revelations' there are hard truths to be learnt. The real question is before us all. Will we learn or will we ignore?

God never wastes words because He wants us to realise the enormous consequences of such broken relationship between the Creator and those whom He created.

Repentance is the preparation of our hearts for God. Before God can build our lives, He must first clear away the debris and clutter. Before He can plant any good seed, He must remove the weeds. Otherwise, we will always be a mixture. The seeds of sin will choke the good seed.

> * 'Repentance Eliminates Our Inner Deviousness, Enabling Us To Be Direct With God.'

Until repentance has done a complete work, we avoid being fully open and direct with God about our need. We hide behind excuses and erect defences to keep ourselves from knowing what is really going on inside. But repentance clears away all lies, and rationalising and we are then able to call sin, sin, allowing God to come to the heart of our need. We welcome His remaking of our inner landscaping.

As we have already discussed – Isaiah 40: 3-4; together with Jeremiah 4:1-4; Repentance cleanses the "land of our heart" from bad seeds.

It is not enough to cut down the bad plants of external sin; the roots must be pulled out and the seeds destroyed. Land which has not been cultivated must be cleansed by repeated ploughing up; once is not enough. Such fallow ground - uncultivated land - must undergo successive ploughing to break up all hard clots and to deeply purge the soil of all remaining seeds dropped by the birds or brought by the wind.

This is just as true concerning our sinful lives as it is for neglected land. The land does not become a desert, but a wilderness. It grows bad seed if not used for good seed.

Repentance is digging down deep to establish foundations on solid rock. An Architectural truth is that "The taller the building, the deeper the foundation."

It remains as true today as it has ever been that the foundation must support the entire structure. For this reason, God – Who is the Creator and foremost Architect – does not attempt to build His new life through Christ Jesus, upon our surface habits alone;

Romans 10:6-9; *"But trusting God to shape the right living in us is a different story—no precarious climb up to heaven to recruit the Messiah, no dangerous descent into hell to rescue the Messiah.*

So, what exactly was Moses saying? The word that saves is right here, as near as the tongue in your mouth, as close as the heart in your chest. It's the word of faith that welcomes God to go to work and set things right for us.

This is the core of our preaching. Say the welcoming word to God—"Jesus is my Master"—embracing, body and soul, God's work of doing in us what he did in raising Jesus from the dead. That's it. You're not "doing" anything; you're simply calling out to God, trusting him to do it for you. That's salvation."

He insists upon stripping us to our base and beginning from scratch, so to speak.

Jeremiah's call as a prophet of repentance emphasises the necessity of the destructive work of God before the building of the new you, can begin.

Jeremiah 1: 9-10; Amplified. *"Then the Lord put forth His hand and touched my mouth, and the Lord said to me, 'Behold, I have put My words in your mouth. See, I have this day appointed you to the oversight of the nations and of the kingdoms, to root out and to pull down, to destroy and to overthrow, to build and to plant."*

* 'Reformation Deals Only With The Surface;

However
Repentance Is A Change Of Heart.'

During the history of the nation Israel, the prophets were constantly calling for a thorough and on-going repentance from idolatry and a return to God.

Under several Kings, Judah experienced reformation. Idols were cut down and certain idolatrous practices - abominations to the Lord - were eliminated; but the people were not turned to God. Their affections were not captivated by Him alone.

While things looked good on the outside, they were doing the same abominations on the inside in subtle, disguised ways.

* 'But God Is Always Concerned With The Heart, The Root Of Our Conduct.'

Sinners can quit smoking and drinking and the like, but this does not make them Christians. It just makes them reformers.

Only the Holy Spirit, creating inner change, can make genuine the promise and intent of God, that we can all become new creatures with an ongoing new creation experiential life, and that can only happen by an attitude of genuine repentance on the part of the sinner and an acceptance of Jesus as the redeemer, the Saviour of our soul.

Hosea, the prophet, paints a vivid picture of the difference between reformation and repentance when he urges the people not to merely plant new seeds, but to plough fresh ground. Prepare the way for God's word.

Hosea 10:12; Amplified. *"Sow for yourselves according to righteousness, upright and right standing with God; reap according to mercy and loving - kindness. Break up your uncultivated ground, for it is time to seek the Lord, to inquire for and of Him and to require, His favour, till He comes and teaches you righteousness and rains His righteous gift of salvation upon you."*

Jesus said much the same thing when He gave the "Parable of the Sower".

Luke 8:9-15; *"A farmer went out to sow his seed. Some of it fell on the road; it was tramped down, and the birds ate it. Other seeds fell in the gravel; it sprouted but withered because it didn't have good roots. Other seeds fell in the weeds; the weeds grew with it and strangled it. Other seed fell in rich earth and produced a bumper crop. "Are you listening to this? Really listening?"*

His disciples asked, "Why did you tell this story?" He said, "You've been given insight into God's kingdom—you know how it works. There are others who need stories. But even with stories some of them aren't going to get it: Their eyes are open but don't see a thing, their ears are open but don't hear a thing. This story is about some of those people.

The seed is the Word of God. The seeds on the road are those who hear the Word, but no sooner do they hear it than the Devil snatches it from them, so they won't believe and be saved.

The seeds in the gravel are those who hear with enthusiasm, but the enthusiasm doesn't go very deep. It's only another fad, and the moment there's trouble it's gone.

And the seed that fell in the weeds—well, these are the ones who hear, but then the seed is crowded out and nothing comes of it as they go about their lives worrying about tomorrow, making money, and having fun. But the seed in the good earth—these are the good-hearts who seize the Word and hold on no matter what, sticking with it until there's a harvest".

The above story needs no other explanation because it tells it as it is, in real life, day to day living, in the here and now, so to speak.

We call it repentance "unto life" because it is just that. We turn from dead works – from the futility of our own efforts – to achieve righteousness.

The story of God is that He has already given to all of humankind His own life. When we truly repent, we are stimulated by this new creation life, and from our innermost being we bring forth fruit of Christ likeness. As a result, we, in our own living, fulfil the purpose of God as found in Genesis 1;

Genesis1:26-31; *"God spoke: 'Let us make human beings in our image, make them reflecting our nature. So, they can be responsible, for the fish in the sea, the birds in the air, the cattle, And, yes, Earth itself, and every animal that moves on the face of Earth.*

God created human beings; He created them godlike, reflecting God's nature. He created them male and female. God blessed them: 'Prosper! Reproduce! Fill Earth! Take charge! Be responsible for fish in the sea and birds in the air, for every living thing that moves on the face of the Earth.'

Then God said, 'I've given you every sort of seed-bearing plant on Earth and every kind of fruit-bearing tree, I have given them to you for food. To all animals and all birds, everything that moves and breathes, I give whatever grows out of the ground for food." And there it was. God looked over everything He had made; it was so good, so very good! It was evening, it was morning— Day Six."

We produce in our own lives, His character. His seed and His life will grow up like Himself. We call this "the fruit of the Spirit." It is the result of our union with Him. Jesus periodically checks the fruit in our lives, just as He did the fig tree:

Matthew 21:18; *"Early the next morning Jesus was returning to the city. He was hungry. Seeing a lone fig tree alongside the road, he approached it anticipating a breakfast of figs. When he got to the tree, there was nothing but fig leaves. He said, 'No more figs from this tree—ever!' The fig tree withered on the spot, a dry stick.*

The disciples saw it happen. They rubbed their eyes, saying, 'Did we really see this? A leafy tree one minute, a dry stick the next?' But Jesus was matter of fact: 'Yes— and if you embrace this kingdom life and don't doubt God, you'll not only do minor feats like I did to the fig tree, but also triumph over huge obstacles."

* 'If Our Root Has Been Changed,
The Results Will Show In The Fruit Of Our Character.'

When we decide to compare the outworking of the deeds of the flesh with the deeds of the Spirit: we soon discover that they are, of themselves, mirrors of the inner self as are illustrated in the following Scriptures, which are guides of the sort of person we are, both in the deeds of the flesh as well as the deeds of the Spirit.

The outworking of the deeds of the flesh:

Galatians 5:17-21; "*For there is a root of sinful self-interest in us that is at odds with a free spirit, just as the free spirit is incompatible with selfishness.*

These two ways of life are antithetical, (directly opposed or contrasted; mutually incompatible) *so that you cannot live at times one way and at times another way according to how you feel on any given day. Why don't you choose to be led by the Spirit and so escape the erratic compulsions of a law-dominated existence?*

* 'After All It Is Always A Matter Of Choice:
Gods Way Or My Way.'

It is obvious what kind of life develops out of trying to get your own way all the time: repetitive, loveless, cheap sex. a stinking accumulation of mental and emotional garbage, frenzied and joyless grabs for happiness, trinket gods, magic-show religion. paranoid loneliness, cutthroat competition. All-consuming-yet-never-satisfied wants. A brutal temper. an impotence to love or be loved. divided homes and divided lives.

Small-minded and lopsided pursuits. the vicious habit of depersonalizing everyone into a rival, uncontrolled and uncontrollable addictions. Ugly parodies of community.

I could go on. This isn't the first time I have warned you; you know. If you use your freedom this way, you will not inherit God's kingdom."

The outworking deeds of the spirit:

Galatians 5:22-26; *"But what happens when we live God's way? He brings gifts into our lives, much the same way that fruit appears in an orchard—things like affection for others, exuberance about life, serenity. We develop a willingness to stick with things, a sense of compassion in the heart, and a conviction that a basic holiness permeates things and people.*

We find ourselves involved in loyal commitments, not needing to force our way in life, able to marshal and direct our energies wisely. Legalism is helpless in bringing this about; it only gets in the way.

Among those who belong to Christ, everything connected with getting our own way and mindlessly responding to what everyone else calls necessities is killed off for good - crucified.

* *'Since This Is The Kind Of Life We Have Chosen, The Life Of The Spirit, Let Us Make Sure That We Do Not Just Hold It As An Idea In Our Heads Or A Sentiment In Our Hearts, But Work Out Its Implications In Every Detail Of Our Lives.'*

That means we will not compare ourselves with each other as if one of us were better and another worse. We have far more interesting things to do with our lives. Each of us is an original."

The two – quite different – fruits; The first is that of the Old Testament LAW –and has embedded within it, the selfish outworking of the flesh. This is the anti and ungodly nature which are birthed in and through the rebellion of Satan.

Its fruit is that which is Satan's personal feud with the God of creation and is illustrated in the continuing conflict between a belief system in the God of Grace and Light, and the god of selfishness and darkness which is upon the earth.

Jesus said this Old Testament Law is fulfilled with the advent of His coming.

The second Fruit is that of the Spirit; Sometimes referred to the 'living of GRACE.'

Non-Christian systems are powerless to produce it: By this fruit there is no law needed because this kind of fruit breaks none of the laws of the old or in essence those of the New Testament either.

The two are contrasted here in Galatians verses 17-21; and 22-23; and they clearly show the old manner of life: Under the Law B.C. – before Christ. And in contrast, – and the new life of Grace A.D. – which Christ gave us by His shed blood as a full and unconditional payment for our sins of the flesh.

    1 Timothy 6:3-10; *"If you have leaders there who teach otherwise, who refuse the solid words of our Master Jesus and this godly instruction, tag them for what they are: ignorant windbags who infect the air with germs of envy, controversy, bad-mouthing, suspicious rumours. Eventually there's an epidemic of backstabbing, and truth is but a distant memory. They think religion is a way to make a fast buck.*
A devout life does bring wealth, but it's the rich simplicity of being yourself before God. Since we entered the world penniless and will leave it penniless, if we have bread on the table and shoes on our feet, that's enough,

But if it's only money these leaders are after, they'll self-destruct in no time. Lust for money brings trouble and nothing but trouble. Going down that path, some lose their footing in the faith completely and live to regret it bitterly ever after."

The second is that of the New Testament of GRACE – which was heralded in with the crucified Christ – and is embedded into selfless nature and attitudes which are Spirit infused. This is the fruit given as a free gift from God, who created us from the very beginning of creation. The Spirit's goal is to produce the fruit of His Spirit in the behaviour of the believer and is only observed as the manifestation – result of His work.

When we refer to the nine "fruit of the spirit" as found in the following Scripture we see very early that there is no law in any part of the history of humankind that forbids this type of fruit being produced.

*Galatians 5:22-23; KJV. *"But The Spirit's Fruit Is: love, joy, peace, patience, kindness, goodness, faithfulness, meekness, self-control. There Is No Law Against Such Things."*

In consideration of the above fruit, it surely is Gods intention that we may all have the desire to live out our lives within the ambit of these nine fruits, in such a way that those with whom we have contact will know that we are Ambassadors of the Living Truth, and His name is Jesus the Son of God.

1. LOVE: (agape) God sheds His own love through us by His Spirit. This is a self-giving love, demonstrated both in devotion to God and in concern for His people.

2. JOY: God's Spirit shares Christ's own joy and gladness with us. That knowing that this inner rejoicing is not dependent on circumstances but gives us the ability to bounce back in resiliency when pressures pile upon us.

3. PEACE: What the world must find in tranquillisers and other artificial means for producing relaxation, the Spirit does within us. This inner peace also makes for concord or harmony in relationships and unity in the assembly.

4. LONGSUFFERING: Longsuffering is exactly that. A better word is perhaps patience or fortitude. It is the ability to endure in expectancy of God's help. It is slowness in avenging ourselves of injuries and forbearance because we hope in God.

5. GENTLENESS: We are obliging and easy to work with because of the Spirit's work in us making us agreeable when many people would be touchy and ornery.

6. GOODNESS: (agathos) This is more than the absence of evil; it is positive virtue. We are morally upright and have the desire and capability bless those around us. It makes us generous in attitude and profitable to the kingdom.

7. FAITH OR FAITHFULNESS: Because we are "at rest" we who we are in Jesus on the inside, through the Spirit's

inworking of firm assurance and confidence toward God, we are able to deal with others in good faith and we are known for faithfulness and truthfulness in all our dealings.

8. MEEKNESS: Meekness is not weakness, or Moses would not have been cited as the meekest man on earth. It is the ability to remain mild, gentle, and forgiving under trying circumstances. It requires more strength than reacting.

9. TEMPERANCE: Self-mastery is the result of discipline, but this is only successful when stimulated by the indwelling Spirit. Self-control grows out of genuine relationship with God through the Spirit.

Chapter 5.

"BECOMING FULLY PERSUADED."

Hebrews 6:1; KJV. *"Therefore, leaving the principles of the doctrine of Christ, let us go on unto perfection; not laying again the foundation of repentance from dead works, and of faith toward God,"*

The key words which give us understanding of this relationship are "from" and "to" or "toward." Notice that it is repentance "from" dead works, and faith "toward" God. These two sides – Repentance and Faith – are of the same coin, namely Justification.

Romans 14:1-8; *"Welcome with open arms fellow believers who don't see things the way you do. And don't jump all over them every time they do or say something you don't agree with—even when it seems that they are strong on opinions but weak in the faith department. Remember, they have their own history to deal with. Treat them gently.*

For instance, a person who has been around for a while might well be convinced that he can eat anything on the table, while another, with a different background, might assume all Christians should be vegetarians and eat accordingly.

But since both are guests at Christ's table, wouldn't it be terribly rude if they fell to criticizing what the other ate or didn't eat? God, after all, invited them both to the table.

Do you have any business crossing people off the guest list or interfering with God's welcome? If there are corrections to be made or manners to be learned, God can handle that without your help. Or, say, one person thinks that some days should be set aside as holy and another thinks that each day is pretty much like any other. There are good reasons either way.

So, each person is free to follow the convictions of conscience. What's important in all this is that if you keep a holy day, keep it for God's sake; if you eat meat, eat it to the glory of God and thank God for prime rib; if you're a vegetarian, eat vegetables to the glory of God and thank God for broccoli.

None of us are permitted to insist on our own way in these matters. It's God we are answerable to—all the way from life to death and everything in between—not each other."

I have heard it explained as Repentance being the negative or preparatory side of the coin and Faith as the positive or receptive side of it. Both repentance and faith are gifts from God, initiated freely, according to His grace. They are inseparable; one cannot exist without the other.

Which comes first, repentance or faith? Logically, turning from something precedes turning to something else.

Experimentally, repentance and faith work hand in hand. Scripture puts them in both orders, depending on the emphasis required by context. It is the same Holy Spirit who creates within us the response of repentance who also creates within us the ability to believe.

1 Thessalonians 1: 8-10; *"The word has gotten around. Your lives are echoing the Master's Word, not only in the provinces but all over the place. The news of your faith in God is out. We don't even have to say anything anymore—you're the message!*

People come up and tell us how you received us with open arms, how you deserted the dead idols of your old life so you could embrace and serve God, the true God.

They marvel at how expectantly you await the arrival of his Son, whom he raised from the dead—Jesus, who rescued us from certain doom."

What then is faith? And what does Scripture say about this vital matter in the lives of believers everywhere?

Faith is a persuasion. The English word, Faith, comes from the Greek word Pistis (Pis-tis) which means "firm persuasion; strong and welcome belief; conviction of the truth of anything."

Ability to believe God requires the faith to both trust His character and to take His Word, as true and reliable.

Faith is vital in forming our response to the persuading work of the Holy Spirit as He enables us to hear God's Word. Such persuasions result in an unshakeable confidence, that God's Word is true.

Acts 20:20-21 *"I didn't skimp or trim in any way. Every truth and encouragement that could have made a difference to you, you got. I taught you out in public and I taught you in your homes, urging Jews and Greeks alike to a radical life-change before God and an equally radical trust in our Master Jesus."*

2 Timothy 1:8-14; *"So don't be embarrassed to speak up for our Master or for me, his prisoner. Take your share of suffering for the Message along with the rest of us. We can only keep on going, after all, by the power of God, who first saved us and then called us to this holy work. We had nothing to do with it. It was all his idea, a gift prepared for us in Jesus long before we knew anything about it.*

But we know it now. Since the appearance of our Saviour, nothing could be plainer: death defeated, life vindicated in a steady blaze of light, all through the work of Jesus.

This is the Message I've been set apart to proclaim as preacher, emissary, and teacher. It's also the cause of all this trouble I'm in. But I have no regrets. I couldn't be more sure of my ground—the One I've trusted in can take care of what he's trusted me to do right to the end.

So, keep at your work, this faith and love rooted in Christ, exactly as I set it out for you. It's as sound as the day you first heard it from me. Guard this precious thing placed in your custody by the Holy Spirit who works in us."

Faith is substance and reality. Faith is not imagination, or the wishing of things into being. It is the conviction of the truth by the inner working of the Holy Spirit, who only persuades us to believe what actually exists. If God gives us the faith for something, we can be sure that in the mind of God, that thing really exists and is as good as ours.

Hebrews 11:1-2;40; *'The fundamental fact of existence is that this trust in God, this faith, is the firm foundation under everything that makes life worth living. It's our handle on what we can't see. The act of faith is what distinguished our ancestors, set them above the crowd.*

It is because of the record which follows the above explanation of Faith, that I now go to the rest of this wonderful exposition of the people of faith which we are encouraged to use as models to follow, so to speak.

Hebrews 11:3-40; *"By faith, we see the world called into existence by God's word, what we see created by what we don't see.* Genesis 1.

BY AN ACT OF FAITH, ABEL brought a better sacrifice to God than Cain. (Genesis 4:4; *'Abel also brought an offering, but from the firstborn animals of his herd, choice cuts of meat. GOD liked Abel and his offering.'*)

It was what he believed, not what he brought, that made the difference. That's what God noticed and approved as righteous. After all these centuries, that belief continues to catch our notice.

BY AN ACT OF FAITH, ENOCH skipped death completely. Genesis 5:22-24; Enoch walked steadily with God. After he had Methuselah, he lived another 300 years, having more sons and daughters. Enoch lived a total of 365 years. Enoch walked steadily with God. And then one day he was simply gone: God took him.'

"They looked all over and couldn't find him because God had taken him." We know on the basis of reliable testimony that before he was taken "he pleased God."

It's impossible to please God apart from faith. And why? Because anyone who wants to approach God must believe both that he exists and that he cares enough to respond to those who seek him.

BY FAITH, NOAH BUILT A SHIP IN THE MIDDLE OF DRY LAND. He was warned about something he couldn't see and acted on what he was told.; The result? His family was saved. His act of faith drew a sharp line between the evil of the unbelieving world and the rightness of the believing world. As a result, Noah became intimate with God. Genesis 6:14 – 8:22;

BY AN ACT OF FAITH, ABRAHAM SAID YES TO GOD'S CALL TO TRAVEL to an unknown place that would become his home. When he left, he had no idea where he was going. Genesis 12:1-3;

By an act of faith, he lived in the country promised him, lived as a stranger camping in tents. Isaac and Jacob did the same, living under the same promise. Abraham did it by keeping his eye on an unseen city with real, eternal foundations—the City designed and built by God.

BY FAITH, BARREN SARAH WAS ABLE TO BECOME PREGNANT, *old woman as she was at the time, because she believed the One who made a promise would do what he said. That's how it happened that from one man's dead and shrivelled loins there are now people numbering into the millions.* Genesis 17:19;

Each one of these people of faith died not yet having in hand what was promised, but still believing. How did they do it? They saw it way off in the distance, waved their greeting, and accepted the fact that they were transients in this world. People who live this way make it plain that they are looking for their true home. If they were homesick for the old country, they could have gone back any time they wanted. But they were after a far better country than that— heaven country. You can see why God is so proud of them and has a City waiting for them.

BY FAITH, ABRAHAM, AT THE TIME OF TESTING, *offered Isaac back to God.* Genesis 22:1-2; *Acting in faith, he was as ready to return the promised son, his only son, as he had been to receive him and this after he had already been told, "Your descendants shall come from Isaac."* — "*After all this, God tested Abraham. God said, "Abraham!" "Yes?" answered Abraham. "I'm listening." He said, "Take your dear son Isaac whom you love and go to the land of*

Moriah. Sacrifice him there as a burnt offering on one of the mountains that I'll point out to you."

Abraham figured that if God wanted to, he could raise the dead. In a sense, that's what happened when he received Isaac back, alive from off the altar.

It was also by his faith in God, and all of His promises, that Abram was able to assure his servants that both he and his son would return from the place of the alter of sacrifice.

BY AN ACT OF FAITH, ISAAC REACHED INTO THE FUTURE as he blessed Jacob and Esau. Genesis 27;

BY AN ACT OF FAITH, JACOB ON HIS DEATHBED BLESSED EACH OF JOSEPH'S SONS in turn, blessing them with God's blessing, not his own—as he bowed worshipfully upon his staff. Genesis 49;

BY AN ACT OF FAITH, JOSEPH, WHILE DYING, PROPHESIED The exodus of Israel, and made arrangements for his own burial. Genesis 50;

BY AN ACT OF FAITH, MOSES' PARENTS HID HIM AWAY for three months after his birth. They saw the child's beauty, and they braved the king's decree. Exodus 1 & 2;

BY FAITH, MOSES, WHEN GROWN, REFUSED THE PRIVILEGES OF THE EGYPTIAN ROYAL HOUSE. The book of exodus tells us much about this man and his faith:

He chose a hard life with God's people rather than an opportunistic soft life of sin with the oppressors.

He valued suffering in the Messiah's camp far greater than Egyptian wealth because he was looking ahead, anticipating the payoff.

By an act of faith, he turned his heel on Egypt, indifferent to the king's blind rage. He had his eye on the One no eye can see and kept right on going.

By an act of faith, he kept the Passover Feast and sprinkled Passover blood on each house so that the destroyer of the firstborn wouldn't touch them.

BY AN ACT OF FAITH, THE NATION OF THE ISRAELITES WALKED THROUGH THE RED SEA *on dry ground.*

LEAD BY JOSHUA THE ISRAELITES, BY FAITH, MARCHED *around the walls of Jericho for seven days, and the walls fell flat.* Joshua 6;

BY AN ACT OF FAITH, RAHAB, THE JERICHO HARLOT, *welcomed the spies and escaped the destruction that came on those who refused to trust God. Joshua 2;*

IT WAS ONLY THROUGH THEIR ACTS OF FAITH, GIDEON, BARAK, SAMSON, JEPHTHAH, DAVID, SAMUEL, THE PROPHETS. ETC. *That they were enabled to overcome kingdoms and made justice work.*

In other words, they took the promises for themselves and as a consequence *they were protected from lions, fires, and sword thrusts, turning disadvantage to advantage, won battles, routed alien armies.*

*Women received their love**d** ones back from the dead. There were those who, under torture, refused to give in and go free, preferring something better: resurrection. Others braved abuse and whips, and, yes, chains and dungeons.*

We have stories of those who were stoned, sawed in two, murdered in cold blood; stories of vagrants wandering the earth in animal skins, homeless, friendless, powerless— the world didn't deserve them! — making their way as best they could on the cruel edges of the world.

Not one of these people, even though their lives of faith were exemplary, got their hands on what was promised. God had a better plan for us: that their faith and our faith would come together to make one completed whole, their lives of faith not complete, apart from ours."

Another expression which always springs to mind when discussing or explaining faith and hope is that we are, "In a state of Anticipated Expectation," when we remain in faith. Faith is a gift from God, and it is The Holy Spirit's influence and ability to place the ability to believe God within our hearts. We cannot work ourselves up into believing Faith. It is not the result of mental gymnastics.

Ephesians 2:7-13; *"Now God has us where he wants us, with all the time in this world and the next to shower grace and kindness upon us in Christ Jesus. Saving is all his idea, and all his work. All we do is trust him enough to let him do it. It's God's gift from start to finish!*

If there was one Scripture that dealt with my confused state B.C. it was this, and I can testify that it was at this time – the absorbing of the truth in this particular verse – that I found the key to the common-sense approach God had crafted for me. I needed to drop-dead to self, so that He could raise me up into a new Creation through His Son Jesus.

* 'Never My Way But His Way.'

We don't play the major role. If we did, we'd probably go around bragging that we'd done the whole thing! No, we neither make nor save ourselves.

The key to success is not in our ability, but in our trust in God, to do what He says we should do, rather than what we think. This so that we don't have a 'look at what I have done' rather than giving God the thanks and the glory for what He has done because of our Faith in Him.

God does both the making and saving. He creates each of us by Christ Jesus to join him in the work he does, the good work he has gotten ready for us to do, work we had better be doing.

In my 2nd book 'Our God of Common-Sense' we see that our God is such a father figure that He wants the best for us.

And with this attitude from the Father Heart of God, we need to comprehend what it is that He desires of us. Therefore, we don't get the answers by theology – man's study of God – but by understanding His 'father's heart' and seeing what he does from a Common- sense perspective.

But don't take any of this for granted. It was only yesterday that you outsiders to God's ways had no idea of any of this, didn't know the first thing about the way God works, hadn't the faintest idea of Christ. You knew nothing of that rich history of God's covenants and promises in Israel, hadn't a clue about what God was doing in the world at large.

This perhaps is the central reason that I enclose within these pages so much of HIStory proclaimed in many verses. I try to never take the Word of God out of its context. And for this I stand assured that as God has given His Word in such a personal letter to me, I can only but give it to you the reader.

Now because of Christ—dying that death, shedding that blood—you who were once out of it altogether are in on everything."

Faith is the response to hearing and in this way, God communicates His thoughts to us, through His Word. He enables us to hear what He is saying through His Spirit in a personal way. He knows us and our needs intimately; because He is our Father God Who knows His relationship with us is secure, even when we have not recognised the reality of our relationship with Him.

It was instilled in me from the earliest time in the Moe New Life Christian Centre that the bible that I own is God's personal message to me and therefore I need to understand what it is saying to me and at the level of my understanding.

John 3:1-21; *"There was a man of the Pharisee sect, Nicodemus, a prominent leader among the Jews. Late one night he visited Jesus and said, "Rabbi, we all know you're a teacher straight from God. No one could do all the God-pointing, God-revealing acts you do if God weren't in on it."*

The need to see and realize, just what He has already done, becomes the opening in our hearts to desire to know Him with a greater sense of intimacy.

Jesus said, 'You're absolutely right. Take it from me: Unless a person is born from above, it's not possible to see what I'm pointing to—to God's kingdom.'

'How can anyone, said Nicodemus, be born who has already been born and grown up? You can't re-enter your mother's womb and be born again. What are you saying with this 'born-from-above' talk?

It is vital to the understanding of who God is, and want He desires such a relationship with us to be, that, we accept that He is all Spirit, and we have a dormant spirit – because of the original sin of Adam and Eve – we must therefore need a renewed spiritual awakening so that the relationship can be realized.

Jesus said, 'You're not listening. Let me say it again. Unless a person submits to this original creation—the wind hovering over the water creation, the invisible moving the visible, a baptism into a new life—it's not possible to enter God's kingdom.
When you look at a baby, it's just that: a body you can look at and touch. But the person who takes shape within is formed by something you can't see and touch—the Spirit— and becomes a living spirit.

So don't be so surprised when I tell you that you have to be 'born from above'—out of this world, so to speak. You know well enough how the wind blows this way and that. You hear it rustling through the trees, but you have no idea where it comes from or where it's headed next.
That's the way it is with everyone 'born from above' by the wind of God, the Spirit of God.'

Nicodemus asked, what do you mean by this? How does this happen?' Jesus said, 'You're a respected teacher of Israel and you don't know these basics? Listen carefully. I'm speaking sober truth to you. I speak only of what I know by experience; I give witness only to what I have seen with my own eyes.

There is nothing secondhand here, no hearsay. Yet instead of facing the evidence and accepting it, you procrastinate with questions. If I tell you things that are plain as the hand before your face and you don't believe me, what use is there in telling you of things you can't see, the things of God? No one has ever gone up into the presence of God except the One who came down from that Presence, the Son of Man.

In the same way that Moses lifted the serpent in the desert so people could have something to see and then believe, it is necessary for the Son of Man to be lifted up and everyone who looks up to him, trusting and expectant, will gain a real life, eternal life.

This is how much God loved the world: He gave his Son, his one and only Son. And this is why: so that no one need be destroyed; by believing in Him, anyone can have a whole and lasting life."

It is only when we understand that we are related to God by spiritual birth that His word becomes alive within us.

It is then possible for us to recognise His grace and mercy toward us. This creates within us the response of believing, of being persuaded that what He is saying is indeed true and is directed to us, just as a loving father would do for his child so God our heavenly father has done. P.T.L.

Romans 10:14-17; "But how can people call for help if they don't know who to trust? And how can they know who to trust if they haven't heard of the One who can be trusted? And how can they hear if nobody tells them?

And how is anyone going to tell them unless someone is sent to do it? That's why Scripture exclaims, A sight to take your breath away! Grand processions of people telling all the good things of God!

But not everybody is ready for this, ready to see and hear and act. Isaiah asked what we all ask at one time or another: "Does anyone care, God? Is anyone listening and believing a word of it?"

The point is, Before you trust, you have to listen. But unless Christ's Word is preached, there's nothing to listen to."

Does faith believe the person or his word? The answer to this question is an emphatic BOTH.

* 'Unless We Depend Upon The Character Of The One Speaking, We Cannot Rely Upon His Word.'

Psalm 138:2; *"I kneel in worship facing your holy temple and say it again: "Thank you!" Thank you for your love, thank you for your faithfulness; Most Holy is your name, most Holy is your Word."*

God and His Word are inseparable. God says that He magnifies His Word even above His name.

Psalm 138:1-6; *"Thank you! Everything in me says "Thank you!" Angels listen as I sing my thanks.*

I kneel in worship facing your holy temple and say it again: "Thank you!" Thank you for your love, thank you for your faithfulness; Most holy is your name, most holy is your Word.

The moment I called out, you stepped in; you made my life large with strength. When they hear what you have to say, GOD, all earth's kings will say "Thank you." They'll sing of what you've done: "How great the glory of GOD!"

And here's why: GOD, high above, sees far below; no matter the distance, he knows everything about us.

Jesus Christ is the Word or expression of God. This means that He in no way misrepresents His Father's character. The Greek word for faith, Pistis, includes both trusting God's character and taking His Word at face value.

Hebrew, however, uses four separate words to express the ideas wrapped up in the one Greek word for faith. These Hebrew words are usually translated "trust." Each one emphasises a different aspect of the work of faith. For example, Faith takes refuge within a person. The Hebrew verb meaning "to take refuge within" brings out the emphasis of the safety or trust.

> Ruth 2:12; *Amplified.* *"The Lord recompense you for what you have done, and a full reward be given you by the Lord, the God of Israel, under Whose wings you have come to take refuge."*

Faith can also mean relying upon someone who is completely trustworthy. In this case the Hebrew verb "to lean upon" refers to a personal reliance upon another. It adds the dimension of abandoning one's self in committal to the care of another. We only lean upon that which we are persuaded is dependable.

 Psalm 56:3-4; Amplified. *"What time am I afraid, I will have confidence and put my trust and reliance on You. By, the help of God, I will praise His Word; on God I lean, rely, and confidently put my trust; I will not fear; what can man who is flesh do to me?"*

Faith can also mean letting go of our burdens into the hands of another. We will only let another take over our concerns when we are convinced, he can handle them better than we can ourselves. The Hebrew verb "to roll upon" extends the idea of committal, emphasising even more our act of relinquishing our concerns to another. In this situation we allow God to take full responsibility for us.

 Psalm 22:8; Amplified. *"He trusts and rolled himself on the Lord, that He would deliver him. Let Him deliver him, seeing that He delights in him!"*

Then in the fourth illustration of the Hebrew understanding of the word Faith we see that the expression frees us from our own efforts and enables us to stay put in God.

The Hebrew verb "to stay upon" brings out the aspect of rest from one's own efforts and response in the knowledge that someone trustworthy is caring for us.

Job: 35:14; Amplified. *"How much less when, missing His righteous judgment on earth, say that you do not see Him, that your cause is before Him, and you are waiting for Him!"*

God does not do everything from long distance, by simple decree. He uses means, very often other people, and circumstances.

Allow me to tell a circumstantial story as testimony to this truth.

THE FIRST MIRACLE: When my wife and I had returned from our nine years of ministry to the people of Western Australia, to Frankston Victoria, I needed to have an operation to remove a tumour, which was causing a lot of discomfort, causing me difficulties when walking and in balance in particular. After the surgery I developed Golden Staff and was apparently close to death.

Nevertheless, with God's help I was in a stage of recovery when I was asked to sing and give testimony at a church in Cranbourne an outer suburb of Melbourne.

THE SECOND MIRACLE: Some five weeks later I was sitting in the Market place of the Frankston Shopping Centre when a man came and talked to me.

He was in the Cranbourne congregation when I gave testimony of what had happened over the years of Ministry – at that time nearly fifteen years serving God – throughout Australia.

The Holy Spirit is the active agent of redemption in the world today. He persuades us by His personal presence, but He uses a number of means to accomplish this. God was using this business man to restart my ministry journey. He offered us the use of the upstairs rooms of his shop overlooking the shopping centre where he would cover all our costs for the first eighteen months. Within weeks we started the first of our Living Waters Family Church's in the appropriately named 'UPPER ROOM.'

God together with the Holy Spirit – and they always work in harmony – uses the preaching of the Word. Through the preaching of God's Word, we are persuaded to believe and turn to God.

THE THIRD MIRACLE: We had no musicians and no instruments other than voices, a set of spoons, and a tambourine. Within just a short period of time we grew to about 20 people, but still no musicians. We prayed for Gods assistance in this matter – my tambourine playing was not the best by an exceptionally long way – and then God acted.

A phone call from a lady in Queensland who had no knowledge of me other than God speaking into her life, and He invited her to donate a piano which was in storage in Melbourne. We said thankyou to both her and the Lord for this provision and had it delivered within days. BUT.

THE FOURTH MIRACLE: We still had no-one to play the piano. I was invited to conduct a Funeral Service for a man who was an ex-serviceman, but who I did not know. (prior to my operation mentioned above I had the honour of being a commissioned Chaplain with the RANR both in West Australia for eight years, Tasmania for two years and finally Victoria for a further two years.)

At that service God spoke to a lady during the service and told her of our situation. At the end of the service, she talked to me and told me what God had put upon her heart. She was a pianist and asked me if we would like to use her ability in our new church. Of course, we said yes please, and thanked God again for His provision.

Faith has been my constant companion since the day of my salvation. I have discovered that I am, who I am, and together in the faith given and expressed through the Holy Spirit, what I endeavour to do, is what God has purposed me to do and is founded upon the following Scriptures: Allow me to explain:

The first was given to me in preparation for what God had planned for the area of ministry which was in the near future – 1979 – to take up a ministry – for a time – in Launceston Tasmania. And although I have written of this earlier in this book, I repeat some of this section again because it has been a foundational experience of God conversing with me in different ways throughout the course of my ministry of some 49 years and counting.

Isaiah 6:1-9; *"In the year that King Uzziah died, I saw the Master sitting on a throne—high, exalted! — and the train of his robes filled the Temple. Angel-seraphs hovered above him, each with six wings. With two wings they covered their faces, with two their feet, and with two they flew. And they called back and forth one to the other, Holy, Holy, Holy is GOD-of-the-Angel-Armies. His bright glory fills the whole earth. The foundations trembled at the sound of the angel voices, and then the whole house filled with smoke.*

I said, "Doom! It's Doomsday! I'm as good as dead! Every word I've ever spoken is tainted— blasphemous even! And the people I live with talk the same way, using words that corrupt and desecrate. And here I've looked God in the face! The King! GOD-of-the-Angel-Armies!"

Then one of the angel-seraphs flew to me. He held a live coal that he had taken with tongs from the altar. He touched my mouth with the coal and said, "Look. This coal has touched your lips. Gone your guilt, your sins wiped out."

And then I heard the voice of the Master: "Whom shall I send? Who will go for us?" I spoke up, "I'll go. Send me!" He said, "Go and tell this people:"

The second was given to me as we – that is Noelene and two of our children – were preparing to go to Western Australia to Minister to the unchurched where-ever God should lead us. God raised some eight small church congregation from our obedience to His call. But it is estimated that over the eight-year journey in W.A. some

600 souls have been added to the Kingdom because of our obedience to that call.

1 Corinthians 1:17-31; *"God didn't send me out to collect a following for myself, but to preach the Message of what he has done, collecting a following for him. He didn't send me to do it with a lot of fancy rhetoric of my own, lest the powerful action at the centre – Christ on the Cross – be trivialized into mere words.*

The Message that points to Christ on the Cross seems like sheer silliness to those hellbent on destruction, but for those on the way of salvation it makes perfect sense.

This is the way God works, and most powerfully as it turns out. It's written, 'I'll turn conventional wisdom on its head, I'll expose so-called experts as crackpots.'

It seems to me that many plans that man has deemed to be of God have been hijacked along the way by the desire to be 'up to date, 'modern' and 'sparkling' and 'with it'. So that the presentation of the Word of God needs to be pepped up, so to speak.

However, in so many cases, such modern methods seems to lose the power and authenticity of the Holy Spirit and replaces it with a professional entertainment setting, taking away from God's Word and the central message of the Gospel, which must be that Jesus has come to set the captive free.

So, where can you find someone truly wise, truly educated, truly intelligent in this day and age? Hasn't God exposed it all as pretentious nonsense?

Since the world in all its fancy wisdom never had a clue when it came to knowing God, God in his wisdom took delight in using what the world considered dumb – preaching, of all things! – to bring those who trust him into the way of salvation.

While Jews clamour for miraculous demonstrations and Greeks go in for philosophical wisdom, we go right on proclaiming Christ, the Crucified. Jews treat this like an anti-miracle—and Greeks pass it off as absurd.

But to us who are personally called by God himself—both Jews and Greeks—Christ is God's ultimate miracle and wisdom all wrapped up in one. Human wisdom is so tinny, so impotent, next to the seeming absurdity of God. Human strength can't begin to compete with God's "weakness."

Take a good look, friends, at who you were when you got called into this life. I don't see many of "the brightest and the best" among you, not many influential, not many from high-society families.

Isn't it obvious that God deliberately chose men and women that the culture overlooks and exploits and abuses, chose these "nobodies" to expose the hollow pretensions of the "somebodies"?

That makes it quite clear that none of you can get by with blowing your own horn before God. Everything that we have—right thinking and right living, a clean slate, and a fresh start comes from God by way of Jesus Christ. That's why we have the saying, "If you're going to blow a horn, blow a trumpet for God."

The Holy Spirit directly works within us to convince us of truth. And it is also The Holy Spirit who works within us to convince us that God is true and that His Word is truth. Just as He turns us from sin in repentance, He turns us to Himself and His Word by giving us faith.

John 16:8-12; Amplified. *"And when He comes, He will convict and convince the world and bring demonstration to it about sin and:*

About righteousness (uprightness of heart and right standing with God) and about judgment:

About sin, because they do not believe in Me [trust in, rely on, and adhere to Me];

About righteousness (uprightness of heart and right standing with God), because I go to My Father, and you will see Me no longer;

About judgment, because the ruler (evil genius, prince) of this world [Satan] is judged and condemned and sentence already is passed upon him.

I have still many things to say to you, but you are not able to bear them or to take them upon you or to grasp them now.

The Holy Spirit makes the Scriptures alive to us. We are persuaded through the reading of the Scriptures, for they are the inspired or God-breathed Word of God, therefore, preparing us for the receiving of the gospel message.

John 5:46-47; Amplified. *"For if you believed and relied on Moses, you would believe and rely on Me, for he wrote about Me [personally]. But if you do not believe and trust his writings, how then will you believe and trust My teachings? [How shall you cleave to and rely on My words?]"*

2Tim. 3:16-17; Amplified. *"Every Scripture is God-breathed (given by His inspiration) and profitable for instruction, for reproof and conviction of sin, for correction of error and discipline in obedience, [and] for training in righteousness (in holy living, in conformity to God's will in thought, purpose, and action), So that the man of God may be complete and proficient, well fitted and thoroughly equipped for every good work."*

The Lord's miracles are meant to help our faith. His miraculous works confirm the supernatural source of His Word, thereby persuading us to believe His claims. Those claims to divine authority are more than authenticated through His signs. Jesus was never afraid to challenge unbelief.

John 10:37-38; Amplified. *"If I am not doing the works [performing the deeds] of My Father, then do not believe Me [do not adhere to Me and trust Me and rely on Me].*

But if I do them, even though you do not believe Me or have faith in Me, [at least] believe the works and have faith in what I do, in order that you may know and understand [clearly] that the Father is in Me, and I am in the Father [One with Him].

There are persuasions which do not originate with the Holy Spirit and God's living Word. Some of these other persuasions may even quote Scripture, but not as God's living Word to us now. We are exposed to many voices and/or impressions. I have heard it said that we hear the world 80% - the devil 15% and God only 5% of time. If we expose our minds, emotions and will to the 95%, we can become convinced of something that is not true.

It is only through our Salvation and New Creation living in the Holy Spirit that we can change the percentages. Truth, you recall, is objective. Something does not become true or factual simply because we believe it.

Presumption is not faith. God warns us against presumption through the severe punishment He inflicted upon those who dared to presume on Him. This word comes from the Latin praesumere which means "to anticipate, suppose, or take in advance." The English definition is much closer to the Bible usage; it means "to dare, to take too much upon one's self."

Presumption by and on the part of man, violates God's holiness and sovereign authority because it is that which was not given to them. They overstep the limits of propriety and courtesy and intrude themselves into places where they have no business. This is not aggressive faith, but blatant rebellion.

Leviticus 9:22-24; *"Aaron lifted his hands over the people and blessed them. Having completed the rituals of the Absolution-Offering, the Whole-Burnt-Offering, and the Peace-Offering, he came down from the Altar. Moses and Aaron entered the Tent of Meeting.*

When they came out, they blessed the people, and the Glory of GOD appeared to all the people. Fire blazed out from GOD and consumed the Whole-Burnt-Offering and the fat pieces on the Altar. When all the people saw it happen, they cheered loudly and then fell down, bowing in reverence.

Leviticus 10:1-3; *"That same day Nadab and Abihu, Aaron's sons, took their censers, put hot coals and incense in them, and offered "strange" fire to GOD—something GOD had not commanded. Fire blazed out from GOD and consumed them—they died in GOD's presence.*

Moses said to Aaron, "This is what GOD meant when he said, To the one who comes near me, I will show myself holy; Before all the people, I will show my glory." Aaron was silent."

The point to make here is that the offerings by Nadab and Abihu were given from a self-conscience – flesh perspective and had no Spiritual and relational accord. It –

simply put, was Not God's way, but rather the ways of man, so to speak.

When we approach our relationship with God, we are beholden to build that relationship according to the very foundations which He the Lord has declared. If we disobey Him in this, we are less than pleasing and will surely pay the price.

Assumption limits faith. Very often we come to situations with our minds already made up. Assumption means the act of taking something for granted or supposing that a thing is true without basis in fact. We are so full of our assumptions or pre-conceived ideas, that we are not really open to hear what God is saying to us now.

We may miss what He is actually doing because we do not see what we expected to see. We may become too rigid in our expectations and thereby limit God.

* 'Presumption Is Dangerous Because It Pre-Empts – It Runs Ahead Of The Plan, Therefore, It Is Unreliable.'
* 'Assumption Limits Faith Because It Has No Ownership Other Than What We Think, Not What We Know.'

Many of the Jews missed their Messiah because of their assumption that He would be a nationalistic, military king who would lead them in throwing off Roman rule. They either did not comprehend or were not prepared to accept a spiritual kingdom.

Chapter 6:

'FAITH IS FOUNDED UPON FACT'

1John 5:1-15; *"Whosoever believes that Jesus is the Christ is born of God: and every one that loves Him who is the Father of the Son, also loves the Father's Son. By this we know that we love the children of God, when we love God, and keep his commandments. For this is the love of God, that we keep his commandments: and his commandments are not grievous. For whatsoever is born of God overcomes the world: and this is the victory that overcomes the world, [even] our faith.*

Who is he that overcomes the world, but he that believes that Jesus is the Son of God? This is he that came by water and blood, [even] Jesus Christ; not by water only, but by water and blood. And it is the Spirit that bears witness because the Spirit is truth. For there are three that bear record in heaven, the Father, the Word, and the Holy Ghost: and these three are one. And there are three that bear witness in earth, the Spirit, and the water, and the blood: and these three agree in one.

If we receive the witness of men, the witness of God is greater: for this is the witness of God which he has testified of his Son.
He that believes on the Son of God has the witness in himself', he that believe not, God hath made him a liar; because he believes not the record that God gave of his Son.

And this is the record that God has given to us eternal life, and this life is in his Son. He that has the Son has life; [and] he that has not the Son of God has not life.

The above passage lets us see that in God's word there is no expression in which His word can be confessed as anything but truth – it is never expressed as of the in-between colour of grey – it is always as it is purposed to be clearly understood – unadulterated Truth.

These things have I written to you that believe on the name of the Son of God; that you may know that you have eternal life, and that you may believe on the name of the Son of God. And this is the confidence that we have in him, that, if we ask any thing according to his will, he hears us: And if we know that he hears us, whatsoever we ask, we know that we have the petitions that we desired of him."

There is an absolute basic tenant to the understanding of Faith and that it is fundamental to the act of redemption. Faith is included among the six foundation stones or first principles of Christ precisely because it is basic. There is no salvation apart from believing upon Christ as the incarnate Son of God.

Faith is God's chosen channel of God's saving grace. By His grace, or unmerited favour, God creates faith within us, enabling us to believe His Word and to rely upon Him as our Saviour. Faith, like repentance, is a gift from God.

Ephesians 2: 8-9; *"By grace you have been saved through faith, and this is not from you, it is the gift of God, nor is it from works, lest anyone should boast."*

Faith is the first step in pleasing God. Faith is not like money; we do not hoard it up and present it to God in order to please Him. We simply allow Him to persuade us that He does indeed exist and that His Word is utterly trustworthy. We please Him by remaining open to His persuading.

Hebrews 11: 6; *".... But without faith it is impossible to please Him, because whoever comes to God must believe that He exists and that He rewards those who seek Him."*

Faith is the only way we gain access to God's holy presence. But for us to come to God by means of the new and living way through Christ, we must exercise faith in His blood because where Sin separates us from God; the Blood of Jesus the Sacrificial Lamb makes a fresh way of approach. We must allow that shed blood to speak peace to our own conscience.

Romans 5: 1-2; *"Therefore, having been justified by faith, we have peace with God through our Lord Jesus Christ, through Whom also by faith we have been led into this grace in which we stand, and we boast about the hope of God's glory."*

Faith is our means of becoming stabilized in the truth. Until we develop a settled and firm conviction of what we believe, we will continue to be blown about by every wind of doctrine.

We only begin to mature after we have personally committed ourselves by a definite decision to believe God's Word.

Our confession of faith regarding Christ qualifies us for other experiences. Incredibly early in the history of the Church, creeds became central within the church because such creeds were accepted as an oath of membership.

Why? A creed – comes from the Latin *credo* which means – statement of faith or confession of one, would believe. Converts were required to verbalize what they believed before they were permitted to be water baptized or to partake of The Lord's Supper.

   Acts 8:37; *"And Philip said, If you believe with all your heart, you may. And he answered and said, 'I believe that Jesus Christ is the Son of God."*

Just as in repentance, all three basic areas of life are touched: Body, Soul, and Spirit. Most people would understand the Body consists of Bone, Blood, and Flesh: However, the Soul and the Spirit are often not so well understood.

The Soul consists of the Mind, Will and Emotion: and the Spirit consists of Conscience, Fellowship, and Intuition. Genuine persuasion creates right thinking about God, consisting of right feeling, definite decisions, and spiritual commitment. In other words, faith activates the whole man.

Right thinking about who God is, allows us to build a concept of God's precepts concerning right relationships both with Him as the Creator and Heavenly Father and this enables us to also have right relationships our fellow humans.

In fact, I believe that, as is our personal relationship with others, so is our relationship with God. This is Biblically expressed as Righteousness: Which means right relations with both God and our fellow man. It is impossible to love God and hate others, at the same time, so to speak.

So therefore the 'Mind' must be informed of the truth, because 'Faith' is more than intellectual assent; it is commitment with knowledge to obey the truth of the gospel.

People cannot believe until they have heard the message or "good news"; this is why preaching, teaching and literature are essential tools given so that the truth which has always been in existence, but hidden because of the darkness of the Sin Factor, can be brought into the light of God's Word.

Romans 10:14-16; *"How then shall they call on him in whom they have not believed? And how shall they believe in him of whom they have not heard? And how shall they hear without a preacher? And how shall they preach, except they are sent? As it is written, 'How beautiful are the feet of them that preach the gospel of peace and bring glad tidings of good things!" But they have not all obeyed the gospel. For Esaias said, Lord, who has believed our report?"*

There is wonderful chorus of absolute simplicity:

And I feel like singing it even as I write these words.

> *"It's such good news that Jesus loves me.*
> *He came and died, that I might live.*
> *My heart rejoices in God my Saviour.*
> *It's such good news that Jesus lives."*

The Will is that central component which sets our actions. It is the will that sets us into motion whether for good or evil, whether positive or negative. We must be mindful that whatever we WILL to do, will have either positive or negative effects both upon us and on others.

Real persuasion results in action. We may think things over and allow our emotions to dwell upon them with delight, but Christ requires obedience, and this is impossible apart from the determination of the will. We must decide to become involved in Christ by doing what He has said to do.

Emotion is recognised through our feelings and our expressions when we are stirred, so to speak, and at a level that prompts us to act – behave – accordingly. Therefore, it is when taken in the context of those 'foundations for

Christian living' that we may express our desires to embrace the truth about Jesus, and what He means to us personally.

* 'Our Heart Response Is Absolutely Essential, For Everything Else Flows Out From Within The Heart.'

Until our affections are embraced – motivated from within the heart – mentally captivated – those feelings may not necessarily lead to change in our lives.

Romans 10: 9-10; KJV. *"That if you shall confess with your mouth the Lord Jesus and shall believe in your heart that God has raised him from the dead, you shall be saved. For with the heart man believes to righteousness; and with the mouth confession is made to salvation."*

The Holy Spirit produces within us the continued ability to believe God and enables us to grow up into His likeness as we persevere in believing. Faith makes us receptive to God. He can enter into us and change us.

John 1:10-14; *"He was in the world, the world was there through him, and yet the world didn't even notice. He came to his own people, but they didn't want him. But whoever did want him, who believed he was who he claimed and would do what he said, He made to be their true selves, their child-of-God selves. These are the God-begotten, not blood-begotten, not flesh-begotten, not sex-begotten. The Word became flesh and blood and moved into the neighborhood.*

We saw the glory with our own eyes, the one-of-a-kind glory, like Father, like Son, Generous inside and out, true from start to finish.

So therefore, we discover that Faith is not based upon human knowledge but is based upon that higher knowledge – the knowledge which comes only from God. However, revelation does not contradict historical and scientific fact when these are based upon reality and are sufficiently complete.

* 'Faith Gives Us A Spiritual Understanding Of All That Is Real.'

Faith rests solidly on truth as God knows it.

Hebrews 11:3; *"Through faith we understand that the worlds were framed by the word of God, so that things which are seen were not made of things which do appear."*

John 17:3; *"And this is life eternal, that they might know You the only true God, and Jesus Christ, whom you have sent."*

Faith is our acceptance of God's truth as it is revealed to us. It is not limited to what can only be learned through our senses and instruments of science. God is Spirit. Some facts about Him can only be spiritually discerned.

Faith is not Gnosticism because a Gnostic relies on knowledge – particularly upon knowledge gleaned from either mystical or religious sources. It of itself has no need to exploring the Faith which comes from a Godly perspective:

Faith is not mystical but historically based upon the truth of the Who, the Why and the How of God in His word. Once more allow me to bring our attention to Biblical examples:

Hebrews 11:1-6; *"The fundamental fact of existence is that this trust in God, this faith, is the firm foundation under everything that makes life worth living. It's our handle on what we can't see.*

The act of faith is what distinguished our ancestors, setting them above the crowd.

By faith, we see the world called into existence by God's word, what we see created by what we don't see.

By an act of faith, Abel brought a better sacrifice to God than Cain. It was what he believed, not what he brought, that made the difference. That's what God noticed and approved as righteous. After all these centuries, that belief continues to catch our notice.

By an act of faith, Enoch skipped death completely. "They looked all over and couldn't find him because God had taken him." We know on the basis of reliable testimony that before he was taken "he pleased God."

It's impossible to please God apart from faith. And why? Because anyone who wants to approach God must believe both that he exists and that he cares enough to respond to those who seek him."

There is no contradiction between matter and Spirit in the Christian faith. God was manifest in the flesh - He took upon Himself a real human body and became subject to the same limitations we all experience as mortals. Christ was historical; He existed at a point in time and space, and he continues to live forever in His resurrected body.

1 John 4:2; *"Hereby you know the Spirit of God: Every spirit that confesses that Jesus Christ is come in the flesh is of God:"*

Faith is not Pragmatism. It does not rely upon just the observable factors: Seeing is not believing, so to speak, but can – where necessary – support evidence of the actions of God. For instance, in the case of Signs, Wonders and Miracles, of which there are more than enough to convinces those whose hearts are not of the Sceptic kind.

Faith therefore is not motivated or powered by any inner or subjective reality alone; but rather it embraces and reacts to objective reality - a God who is there and whose words are truth. Faith is valid not because it is self-authenticating through personal; awareness, but because God's record concerning his Son is reliable.

Faith is our reaction to something - or Someone - very real, leading to positive living in Body, Soul, and Spirit. In other words, Faith produces right conduct.

1 John 4:1-6; *"My dear friends, don't believe everything you hear. Carefully weigh and examine what people tell you. Not everyone who talks about God comes from God. There are a lot of lying preachers loose in the world. Here's how you test for the genuine Spirit of God.*

Everyone who confesses openly his faith in Jesus Christ—the Son of God, who came as an actual flesh-and-blood person—comes from God and belongs to God. And everyone who refuses to confess faith in Jesus has nothing in common with God. This is the spirit of antichrist that you heard was coming.

Well, here it is, sooner than we thought! My dear children, you come from God and belong to God.
You have already won a big victory over those false teachers, for the Spirit in you is far stronger than anything in the world. These people belong to the Christ-denying world. They talk the world's language, and the world eats it up.

But we come from God and belong to God. Anyone who knows God understands us and listens. The person who has nothing to do with God will, of course, not listen to us. This is another test for telling the Spirit of Truth from the spirit of deception."

  When we put the Soul and the Spirit together: The Soul consisting of the Mind, Will and Emotion: and the Spirit consisting of Conscience, Fellowship, and Intuition we come out with changed behaviour. For this reason, we are able to live differently:

Faith creates experiences which are credentials to believers: The strongest credential for a believer is his own changed life. He has become a living epistle. It is written in his heart that God is faithful.

1 John 4:7-9; *"My beloved friends, let us continue to love each other since love comes from God. Everyone who loves is born of God and experiences a relationship with God. The person who refuses to love doesn't know the first thing about God, because God is love—so you can't know him if you don't love.*
This is how God showed his love for us: God sent his only Son into the world so we might live through him."

We experience the reality of the gospel in three distinct ways:

a. The blood sacrifice of Jesus our Savour, for the cleansing and forgiveness of all sin.

b. The waters of Baptism, through which we make a tangible commitment to follow in the ways of Jesus our Lord.

c. The empowering of the Holy Spirit which enables us to do the works of the ministry promised to all who believe by Faith in Him.

Faith creates an internal witness that brings alive the very essence of God – an awareness that we are His and He is ours – through the right relationship with Him our 'Father Heart' of all creation.

1 John 4:10-13; *"This is the kind of love we are talking about—not that we once upon a time loved God, but that he loved us and sent his Son as a sacrifice to clear away our sins and the damage they've done to our relationship with God.*

My dear, dear friends, if God loved us like this, we certainly ought to love each other. No one has seen God, ever. But if we love one another, God dwells deeply within us, and his love becomes complete in us—perfect love! This is how we know we're living steadily and deeply in him, and he in us: He's given us life from his life, from his very own Spirit.'

We experience a genuine spiritual birth and become new people. It brings us into the realm of the 'CAN DO PEOPLE OF GOD'

'We Can Love Other Believers.
We Can Keep God's Commandments.
We Can Even Overcome The Present World System.'

Paul describes the effect of this witness in producing inner assurance regarding our relationship with God. We truly are His children, and we know it, therefore we have a deep sense of belonging, so to speak.

Romans 8:14-17; *"God's Spirit beckons. There are things to do and places to go! This resurrection life you received*

from God is not a timid, grave-tending life. It's adventurously expectant, greeting God with a childlike "What's next, Papa?" God's Spirit touches our spirits and confirms who we really are. We know who he is, and we know who we are: Father and children. And we know we are going to get what's coming to us—an unbelievable inheritance!
We go through exactly what Christ goes through. If we go through the hard times with him, then we're certainly going to go through the good times with him!

* 'Faith Is The Proof Of The Confidence
We Have In Him And Therefore, His Word.'

1 John 4:12-21; *"No one has seen God, ever. But if we love one another, God dwells deeply within us, and his love becomes complete in us—perfect love! This is how we know we're living steadily and deeply in him, and he in us: He's given us life from his life, from his very own Spirit.*

Also, we've seen for ourselves and continue to state openly that the Father sent his Son as Savior of the world. Everyone who confesses that Jesus is God's Son participates continuously in an intimate relationship with God.

We know it so well, we've embraced it heart and soul, this love that comes from God. God is love. When we take up permanent residence in a life of love, we live in God and God lives in us.

This way, love has the run of the house, becomes at home, and matures in us, so that we're free of worry on Judgment Day—our standing in the world is identical with Christ's.
There is no room in love for fear. Well-formed love banishes fear. Since fear is crippling, a fearful life — fear of death, fear of judgment — is one not yet fully formed in love.

We, though, are going to love—love and be loved. First, we were loved, now we love. He loved us first. If anyone boasts, "I love God," and goes right on hating his brother or sister, thinking nothing of it, he is a liar. If he won't love the person he can see, how can he love the God he can't see?

The command we have from Christ is blunt: Loving God includes loving people. You've got to love both."

The beautiful position in which we find ourselves, as believers in Him, is that we can have absolute assurance – belief – that our prayers are answered because God is there to hear them and to act upon our petitions when we pray in accordance with His purposes.

It is in this knowledge – we must pray according to His will to be heard – lifting our prayer out of the realm of the 'ifs' and the 'maybe's', so to speak, and into the power of His Word.

* 'Our Reliance Is Not Upon Our Great Prayers
But Upon Our Great God.'

Chapter 7:

"THE RIGHTEOUSNESS OF FAITH."

Romans 4:1-8; *"So how do we fit what we know of Abraham, our first father in the faith, into this new way of looking at things? If Abraham, by what he did for God, got God to approve him, he could certainly have taken credit for it. But the story we're given is a God-story, not an Abraham-story. What we read in Scripture is, "Abraham entered into what God was doing for him, and that was the turning point. He trusted God to set him right instead of trying to be right on his own." If you're a hard worker and do a good job, you deserve your pay; we don't call your wages a gift. But if you see that the job is too big for you, that it's something only God can do, and you trust him to do it—you could never do it for yourself no matter how hard and long you worked—well, that trusting-him-to-do-it is what gets you set right with God, by God. Sheer gift.*

This section of Scripture must become the rule of thumb, so to speak, for all Christian living, and I can testify and witness that the truth in the above section – verses 3-5 – has had and continues to have, a profound effect within my own walk, In Him.

David confirms this way of looking at it, saying that the one who trusts God to do the putting-everything-right without insisting on having a say in it is one fortunate man: Fortunate those whose crimes are carted off, whose sins are wiped clean from the slate. Fortunate is the person against whom the Lord does not keep score."

Romans 4:13-25; *"That famous promise God gave Abraham—that he and his children would possess the earth—was not given because of something Abraham did or would do. It was based on God's decision to put everything together for him, which Abraham then entered when he believed. If those who get what God gives them only get it by doing everything they are told to do and filling out all the right forms properly signed, that eliminates personal trust completely and turns the promise into an ironclad contract! That's not a holy promise; that's a business deal. A contract drawn up by a hard-nosed lawyer and with plenty of fine print only makes sure that you will never be able to collect.*

* 'Religiosity And Churchianity are Man's Way To Their god, Whatever That May Be.
Christianity Is God's Way For Man To Build A Lasting Relationship With Him, Through Jesus His Only Begotten Son.'

But if there is no contract in the first place, simply a promise—and God's promise at that—you can't break it. This is why the fulfillment of God's promise depends entirely on trusting God and his way, and then simply embracing him and what he does.

God's promise arrives as pure gift. That's the only way everyone can be sure to get in on it, those who keep the religious traditions and those who have never heard of them. For Abraham is father of us all. He is not our racial father—that's reading the story backwards.

He is our faith father. We call Abraham "father" not because he got God's attention by living like a saint, but because God made something out of Abraham when he was nobody.

Isn't that what we've always read in Scripture, God saying to Abraham, "I set you up as father of many people's"? Abraham was first named "father" and then became a father because he dared to trust God to do what only God could do: raise the dead to life, with a word make something out of nothing. When everything was hopeless, Abraham believed anyway, deciding to live not on the basis of what he saw he couldn't do but on what God said he would do. And so, he was made father of a multitude of peoples.

God himself said to him, "You're going to have a big family, Abraham!" Abraham didn't focus on his own impotence and say, "It's hopeless. This hundred-year-old body could never father a child." Nor did he survey Sarah's decades of infertility and give up. He didn't tiptoe around God's promise asking cautiously skeptical questions. He plunged into the promise and came up strong, ready for God, sure that God would make good on what he had said. That's why it is said, "Abraham was declared fit before God by trusting God to set him right."

But it's not just Abraham; it's also us! The same thing gets said about us when we embrace and believe the One who brought Jesus to life when the conditions were equally hopeless. The sacrificed Jesus made us fit for God, set us right with God."

The righteousness God demands from man is clearly set down in the Law. If man could keep the entire law without one slip, he would be righteous – in right standing with God. The challenge is that man is unable to keep the law.

That man is totally depraved, is in essence saying, that by his or her own unaided efforts he cannot fulfil all of God's commands. The law is a totality. If the entire law is not kept, none of it is kept. God considers righteousness as keeping the law as a whole – it is all or nothing – so to speak. The reality is therefore, if, or when, we break any of the law, we have broken the whole law.

James 2:10; *"For whosoever shall keep the whole law, and yet offend in one [point], he is guilty of all."*

* 'God Gave Us The Law So That We Could Measure
Our Own Inability
And Therefore, Our Need Of A Saviour.'

Romans 7:7; *"But I can hear you say, "If the law code was as bad as all that, it's no better than sin itself." That's certainly not true. The law code had a perfectly legitimate function. Without its clear guidelines for right and wrong, moral behaviour would be mostly guesswork. Apart from* the succinct, surgical command, "You shall not covet," I could have dressed covetousness up to look like a virtue and ruined my life with it.

Man possesses nothing good within himself.

Romans 7:17-25; *"But I need something more! For if I know the law but still can't keep it, and if the power of sin within me keeps sabotaging my best intentions, I obviously need help! I realize that I don't have what it takes. I can will it, but I can't do it. I decide to do good, but I don't really do it; I decide not to do bad, but then I do it anyway. My decisions, such as they are, don't result in actions. Something has gone wrong deep within me and gets the better of me every time. It happens so regularly that it's predictable. The moment I decide to do good, sin is there to trip me up.*

I truly delight in God's commands, but it's pretty obvious that not all of me joins in that delight. Parts of me covertly rebel, and just when I least expect it, they take charge. I've tried everything and nothing helps. I'm at the end of my rope. Is there no one who can do anything for me? Isn't that the real question?

The answer, thank God, is that Jesus Christ can and does. He acted to set things right in this life of contradictions where I want to serve God with all my heart and mind but am pulled by the influence of sin to do something totally different."

* 'God Has Found No One Righteous,

But We Are All Equally In Need
Of The Gift Of Righteousness.'

Romans 3:9-12; *"So where does that put us? Do we Jews get a better break than the others? Not really. Basically, all of us, whether insiders or outsiders, start out in identical conditions, which is to say that we all start out as sinners. Scripture leaves no doubt about it:*
There's nobody living right, not even one, nobody who knows the score, nobody alert, for God. They've all taken the wrong turn; they've all wandered down blind alleys. No one's living right; I can't find a single one."

The law makes us aware – and this is so very personal – of our sin and declares our guilt as legal fact.

Romans 3:19-22; *"This makes it clear, doesn't it, that whatever is written in these Scriptures is not what God says about others but to us to whom these Scriptures were addressed in the first place! And it's clear enough, isn't it, that we're sinners, every one of us, in the same sinking boat with everybody else?*

Our involvement with God's revelation doesn't put us right with God. What it does is force us to face our complicity in everyone else's sin. But in our time, something new has been added. What Moses and the prophets witnessed to all those years has happened. The God-setting-things-right that we read about has become Jesus-setting-things-right for us. And not only for us, but for everyone who believes in Him. For there is no difference between us and them, in this."

We are only reconciled or restored to right standing through the work of Christ, as by faith we identify ourselves with Him. This faith is based on a thorough turning away from self-reliance and dead works to a complete trust in the work of another, Christ Jesus the Lord.

Romans 3:23-26; *"Since we've compiled this long and sorry record as sinners (both us and them) and proved that we are utterly incapable of living the glorious lives God wills for us, God did it for us.*

Out of sheer generosity he put us in right standing with himself. A pure gift. He got us out of the mess we're in and restored us to where he always wanted us to be. And he did it by means of Jesus Christ. God sacrificed Jesus on the altar of the world to clear that world of sin. Having faith in him sets us in the clear.

God decided on this course of action in full view of the public—to set the world in the clear with himself through the sacrifice of Jesus, finally taking care of the sins he had so patiently endured. This is not only clear, but it's now— this is current history! God sets things right. He also makes it possible for us to live in his rightness."

In coming to grips, so to speak, concerning our personal 'Repentance from dead works', we must consider just one basic factor, we must have faith toward God, before accepting Christ's work on the Cross for us. So, to the extent that we have repented of dead works we have become born again, not through our efforts, but by the price paid for us through the Blood merit of Jesus, who without sin died in our place thereby redeeming us from the penalty of the Law.

Instead of working to merit righteousness, we agree with God that it is impossible. Then we accept His alternative which is to credit us with the righteousness of Christ.

Romans 4:3; KJV. *"For what is written in the scripture? Abraham believed God, and it was counted unto him for righteousness."*

Throughout the Old Testament, God prepared His people for His provision of Christ for justification. Each time men sinned, they were to bring a sacrifice; usually a bull, a sheep or lamb, or goat. The blood of the animal was given as an offering, and sin was covered. But since sin was only covered, not taken away, these sacrifices were often repeated and did not grant complete access into God's presence. Sin requires the shedding of blood, either the death of the sinner or of a substitute.

Hebrews 9:18-28; *"Even the first plan required a death to set it in motion. After Moses had read out all the terms of the plan of the law—God's "will"— he took the blood of sacrificed animals and, in a solemn ritual, sprinkled the* document and the people who were its beneficiaries. And then he attested its validity with the words, "This is the blood of the covenant commanded by God." He did the same thing with the place of worship and its furniture.

Moses said to the people, "This is the blood of the covenant God has established with you." Practically everything in a will hinges on a death. That's why blood, the evidence of death, is used so much in our tradition, especially regarding forgiveness of sins. That accounts for the prominence of blood and death in all these secondary practices that point to the realities of heaven. It also accounts for why, when the real thing takes place, these animal sacrifices aren't needed anymore, having served their purpose.

For Christ didn't enter the earthly version of the Holy Place; he entered the Place Itself and offered himself to God as the sacrifice for our sins.

He doesn't do this every year as the high priests did under the old plan with blood that was not their own; if that had been the case, he would have to sacrifice himself repeatedly throughout the course of history. But instead, he sacrificed himself once and for all, summing up all the other sacrifices in this sacrifice of himself, the final solution of sin.

Everyone has to die once, then face the consequences. Christ's death was also a one-time event, but it was a sacrifice that took care of sins forever. And so, when he *next appears, the outcome for those eager to greet him is, precisely, salvation."*

However, in the times of the New Testament the sin of man was removed, just like the Garbage Truck that comes and removes the rubbish from my home, I no longer have to live with it at my address.

Not until Christ became the perfect Lamb of God through His death on the cross – as the substitute – for me and you, did He remove sin forever and make possible not only that righteous Sonship relationship with God and His dealings with man, but also gave to us the Robe of Righteousness:

Yes, another chorus comes to mind at this time:

"Behold what manner of love the Father has given unto us. Behold what manner of love the Father has given unto us. That we should be called the Sons of God. That we should be called the Sons of God."

*I do not know the Author but nevertheless I give glory to God. P.B.

Some important factors concerning God's own righteousness are:

God is consistent in His dealings with us as individuals: Unity comes through a personal agreement to be together, and we see that it is also the same with God's consistent desire to have such a right-relationship with us – and that in the unity of His Son and us – as individuals.

Thus, our God is desiring a personal identifying factor to make the family complete.

One of the major truth I learnt, as a new Christian, was that His Word is written for me, for my benefit, for my fulfilment in sonship with Him, as if He is my own Father – because in reality – HE IS THAT, AND MORE.

GOD does not show partiality or respect any person: It is not the colour of our skin, for we all have red blood in our veins. It matters not whether we are male or female, for He made each of us in His own image and likeness.

GOD does not set aside His law on a whim or in an inconsistent manner: Therefore, there is a consistency in the principles He has laid down – there are no rules of law that prohibits following any of His guidelines in any country upon earth – as our means of living in unity.

GOD has given us those principles – in the frame of laws – as an expression of His own personal character: Therefore, such principles found in:

Galatians 5:22-23; *"But what happens when we live God's way? He brings gifts into our lives, much the same way that fruit appears in an orchard—things like affection for others, exuberance about life, serenity.*

We develop a willingness to stick with things, a sense of compassion in the heart, and a conviction that a basic holiness permeates things and people.

We find ourselves involved in loyal commitments, not needing to force our way in life, able to marshal and direct our energies wisely. Legalism is helpless in bringing this about; it only gets in the way. they are the embodiment and the revelation of His perfect holiness."

GOD is not above or outside those matters: He has framed them in such a way that – from His perspective – the law is simply the judicial or legal manifestation of what He is.

* 'God Can Never Change Or Deny Himself, And It Is Written That His Desire For You And Me Is That We Should Regain Our Status IN HIM Through Believing In His Son Jesus. This We Call The New Creation Life.'

2 Corinthians 5:14-18; *"Christ's love has moved me to such extremes. His love has the first and last word in everything we do. Our firm decision is to work from this focused centre: One man died for everyone. That puts everyone in the same boat. He included everyone in his death so that everyone could also be included in his life, a resurrection life, a far better life than people ever lived on their own.*

Because of this decision we don't evaluate people by what they have or how they look. We looked at the Messiah that way once and got it all wrong, as you know.

We certainly don't look at him that way anymore. Now we look inside, and what we see is that anyone united with the

Messiah gets a fresh start, is created new. The old life is gone; a new life burgeons! Look at it! All this comes from the God who settled the relationship between us and him, and then called us to settle our relationships with each other."

The law demands the shedding of blood (death) in payment for sin.

Ezekiel 18:4; *"Every soul—man, woman, child—belongs to me, parent, and child alike. You die for your own sin, not another's."*

God's wrath – righteous indignation – is the expression of His holiness and His righteousness. He must react against sin by demanding penalty and payment in full- expiation.

God decreed that since the life is in the blood. So therefore, the payment for sin would be the shedding of blood. Either the person who sinned must die or he could present a substitute.

Christ came to earth to die as our substitute. His death completely satisfied God's penalty and payment for sin. Since He paid in our place, we call Him our victorious substitute.

God gave His Son Jesus as the delegated payment for our sin.

1 Peter 3:18; *"For Christ also has once suffered for sins, the just for the unjust, that he might bring us to God, being put to death in the flesh, but quickened by the Spirit:"*

Peace with God is only possible when His personal wrath is appeased. Sin is not simply a legal matter; it is a personal insult to God. Sin is dealt with through the legal satisfaction or payment; indeed, the debt has – past tense – been paid.

Propitiation means to deal through payment for offence or misdeed allowing the restoration of personal relationship, between the sinner, on the one hand, and God the other.

Restoring God's favour is always that which God desires and is an unconditional relationship endeavour in which we must also be a willing participant. The suffering of Christ, our substitute, placates God's wrath, giving Him a way to release us from punishment through granting pardon or forgiveness.

The propitiation of Christ is pictured by the Old Testament Mercy Seat, which was upon the lid of the Ark of the Covenant. God considered the Mercy Seat His place of meeting His people. Underneath was the broken law, but it was covered over by the sprinkled blood of sacrifice.

Romans 3:21-26; *"But in our time, something new has been added. What Moses and the prophets witnessed to all those years has happened.*

The God-setting-things-right that we read about has become Jesus-setting-things-right for us. And not only for us, but for everyone who believes in him. For there is no difference between us and them in this.

Since we've compiled this long and sorry record as sinners (both us and them) and proved that we are utterly incapable of living the glorious lives God wills for us, God did it for us. Out of sheer generosity he put us in right standing with himself. A pure gift. He got us out of the mess we're in and restored us to where he always wanted us to be. And he did it by means of Jesus Christ. God sacrificed Jesus on the altar of the world to clear that world of sin. Having faith in him sets us in the clear.

God decided on this course of action in full view of the public—to set the world in the clear with himself through the sacrifice of Jesus, finally taking care of the sins he had so patiently endured. This is not only clear, but it's now—this is current history! God sets things right. He also makes it possible for us to live in his rightness."

* 'Justification Means That We Are Legally Declared In Right Standing With God. Explaining This Wonderful Truth Is To Say;
Just As If I Had Never Sinned.'

Justification is God's legal action to reconcile sinners to Himself. It does not set aside the law or violate His holy character in any way. God simply declares that since Christ has fully satisfied the law's demands, God is now free to restore man to right standing on the basis of what Christ has done, under His authority.

Instead of holding us accountable for our sins, God deliberately charged all sin to Christ's account, leaving us free from both guilt and penalty.

Therefore, all that is required of us to receive credit for Christ's righteousness, and to transfer our guilt to Him, is our repentance and faith. Together – confession and repentance – these make possible the application of justification to us.

We are restored to friendship with God.

James 2:23; KJV. *"And the scripture was fulfilled which said, 'Abraham believed God,' and it was imputed unto him for righteousness: and he was called the Friend of God."*

We stand legally declared righteous.

Galatians 3:5-6; *"Answer this question: Does the God who lavishly provides you with his own presence, his Holy Spirit, working things in your lives you could never do for yourselves, does he do these things because of your strenuous moral striving or because you trust him to do them in you? Don't these things happen among you just as they happened with Abraham? He believed God, and that act of belief was turned into a life that was right with God."*

Imputation is a legal decree or transaction. The imputation of righteousness refers to a system of divine bookkeeping by which sin, or righteousness, may be transferred from one person's account to another's.

This principle is behind the whole idea of vicarious sacrifice and justification by faith. When God justifies us through our faith in Christ, He does not impute or account or reckon our sins to us any longer, but transfers this to Christ's account.

It becomes fact because God declares it to be His decision.

Romans 5:18-21; *"Here it is in a nutshell: Just as one person did it wrong and got us in all this trouble with sin and death, another person did it right and got us out of it. But more than just getting us out of trouble, he got us into life!*

* *'One Man Said No To God And Put Many People In The Wrong; One Man Said Yes To God And Put Many In The Right.'*

All that passing laws against sin did was produce more lawbreakers. But sin didn't, and doesn't, have a chance in competition with the aggressive forgiveness we call grace. When it's sin versus grace, grace wins hands down.

All sin can do is threaten us with death, and that's the end of it. Grace, because God is putting everything together again through the Messiah, invites us into life—a life that goes on and on and on, world without end."

The righteousness of God is first of all His own character: it includes both His internal consistency and His fairness or justice in all His dealings.

As I have written earlier in this book, Righteousness is applied to man as "right standing" with God in terms of covenant relationship. It is therefore of vital importance to realise that there is no understanding of righteousness apart from understanding: What the covenant in fact really is. What it means. What it accomplishes and to whom is it relevant.

The Old Testament teaches that righteousness on the part of either God or man consists of fulfilling the promises contained in the covenant or agreement between them.

* 'Righteousness Is A Gift From God To Mankind And It Can Only Be Received By Faith.'

Here comes another favourite Chorus which I love to sing:

'I am covered over with the robe of righteousness,
that Jesus gives to me, gives to me.
I am covered over with the precious blood of Jesus,
and He lives in me, Lives in me.
What a joy it is to know my heavenly father
loves me so and gives to me my Jesus.
When He looks at me, He sees not what I used to be,
but He sees Jesus.'

Praise and Worship No. 235:
Copyright unknown, but all praise to the original author GOD; P.T.

It clothes the believer like a garment making him acceptable in God's sight, while God works on the inside by the Holy Spirit to change his character until he too is right and fair in all his dealings.

God Himself becomes our righteousness: Therefore, it is Jesus Christ who became the gift of righteousness from God to us.

1 Corinthians 1:18-21; *"The Message that points to Christ on the Cross seems like sheer silliness to those hellbent on destruction, but for those on the way of salvation it makes perfect sense. This is the way God works, and most powerfully as it turns out.*

It's written, I'll turn conventional wisdom on its head, I'll expose so-called experts as crackpots.

So where can you find someone truly wise, truly educated, truly intelligent in this day and age? Hasn't God exposed it all as pretentious nonsense?

Since the world in all its fancy wisdom never had a clue when it came to knowing God, God in his wisdom took delight in using what the world considered dumb — preaching, of all things! — to bring those who trust him into the way of salvation."

There are no degrees of righteousness in redemption because God has reduced us all to the same level: we are sinners apart from the gift of Christ. The reason for this 'legal declaration' is to eliminate the boasting which has become natural to man.

The righteousness of God describes our change of position in relation to God. We have right standing with God, on one basis only: we are 'in Christ.'

We are no longer approaching Him on our own merits, which are repugnant to God, but our acceptance is in His beloved Son alone. We receive this new position of right standing by faith when we agree with God that even our best is worthless, and we need to rest our entire weight (of sin) upon Christ.

In my B.C. years I strived to do well, to be important, and to be all the things that would give me what I lacked: Stability, Acceptance, Recognition, Prestige, and the list could go on and on. But alas I always fell short of my goals, such as they were.

It was not until I encountered the Good News of what Jesus had given – for me – so that I could aspire, with that 'Anticipated Expectation,' to be what God had created me to be, and all of this by accepting Him and His Word, and therefore not having to strive without any satisfactions, as I had done, so many times in those 37years without knowing Him.

The following passage – although lengthy – is another personal message given into my life that is a continuing Gift, from He who has always loved me, despite the many sins in my life.

* 'God Loves Me The Sinner But Never The Sin That I Have Continually Committed.'

Philippians 3:7-21; *"The very credentials these people are waving around as something special, I'm tearing up and throwing out with the trash—along with everything else I used to take credit for. And why? Because of Christ.*

Yes, all the things I once thought were so important are gone from my life. Compared to the high privilege of knowing Christ Jesus as my Master, firsthand, everything I once thought I had going for me is insignificant—dog dung. I've dumped it all in the trash so that I could embrace Christ and be embraced by him. I didn't want some petty, inferior brand of righteousness that comes from keeping a list of rules when I could get the robust kind that comes from trusting Christ—God's righteousness.

I gave up all that inferior stuff so I could know Christ personally, experience his resurrection power, be a partner in his suffering, and go all the way with him to death itself. If there was any way to get in on the resurrection from the dead, I wanted to do it.

I'm not saying that I have this all together, that I have it made. But I am well on my way, reaching out for Christ, who has so wondrously reached out for me. Friends don't get me wrong: By no means do I count myself an expert in all of this, but I've got my eye on the goal, where God is beckoning us onward—to Jesus. I'm off and running, and I'm not turning back.

So, let's keep focused on that goal, those of us who want everything God has for us.

If any of you have something else in mind, something less than total commitment, God will clear your blurred vision—you'll see it yet! Now that we're on the right track, let's stay on it. Stick with me, friends. Keep track of those you see running this same course, headed for this same goal.

There are many out there taking other paths, choosing other goals, and trying to get you to go along with them. I've warned you of them many times; sadly, I'm having to do it again. All they want is easy street. They hate Christ's Cross. But easy street is a dead-end street. Those who live there make their bellies their gods; belches are their praise; all they can think of is their appetites.

But there's far more to life for us. We're citizens of high heaven! We're waiting the arrival of the Saviour, the Master, Jesus Christ, who will transform our earthy bodies into glorious bodies like his own. He'll make us beautiful and whole with the same powerful skill by which he is putting everything as it should be, under and around him."

Laying the foundation stone of faith toward God, means accepting the righteousness of God. because it is by faith that we agree with God's decree that we are in right standing with Him on the basis of Christ's work on our behalf. This allows God to work a total change of character in us.

He must first apply the blood to us before He can move in to remake us by the Holy Spirit. This gradual process of conforming us to His likeness in character is called sanctification. Little by little God gives Himself to us as practical righteousness. All this is only possible because of the initial act of declared righteousness, or justification.

It is done as we co-operate in a continuing faith through the Blood of Jesus and with the power of the Holy Spirit.

2 Corinthians 5:21; KJV. *"For he hath made him [to be] sin for us, who knew no sin; that we might be made the righteousness of God in him."*

Chapter Eight.
"FAITH THAT WORKS".

Paul gives us a broad sense of FAITH in the following passage:

Romans 5:1-11; *"By entering through faith into what God has always wanted to do for us—set us right with him, make us fit for him—we have it all together with God because of our Master Jesus.*

The essence of Grace is found in God's Abounding Grace, and we have been given this wonderful gift at the very beginning of our journey out from the darkness and into His glorious kingdom full of His love and our desire to be 'at one' – atonement – with Him by faith in the fulfilment of the sacrifice made by Jesus on the cross for our redemption.

And that's not all: We throw open our doors to God and discover at the same moment that he has already thrown open his door to us. We find ourselves standing where we always hoped we might stand—out in the wide-open spaces of God's grace and glory, standing tall and shouting our praise.

There's more to come: We continue to shout our praise even when we're hemmed in with troubles, because we know how troubles can develop passionate patience in us, and how that patience in turn forges the tempered steel of virtue, keeping us alert for whatever God will do next.

There is no need to ask God for patience because patience is a normal part of our growing into the family and God will always meet the need thereof.

However, there is a note of caution because, there is a distinct difference between our carnal expectation of patience – which is more often than not, a pressure of our emotional state – and the Spiritual patience – which is given by God through the Holy Spirit and is that through which we are strengthened for whatever may lay ahead of us, in this new and living relationship between us and our God.

In alert expectancy such as this, we're never left feeling short-changed. Quite the contrary—we can't round up enough containers to hold everything God generously pours into our lives through the Holy Spirit!

* *'Christ Arrives Right On Time To Make This Happen.*
He Didn't, And Doesn't, Wait For Us To Get Ready.'

He presented himself for this sacrificial death when we were far too weak and rebellious to do anything to get ourselves ready. And even if we hadn't been so weak, we wouldn't have known what to do anyway. We can understand someone dying for a person worth dying for, and we can understand how someone good and noble could inspire us to selfless sacrifice.

But God put his love on the line for us by offering his Son in sacrificial death while we were of no use whatever to him.

Now that we are set right with God by means of this sacrificial death, the consummate blood sacrifice, there is no longer a question of being at odds with God in any way. If, when we were at our worst, we were put on friendly terms with God by the sacrificial death of his Son, now that we're at our best, just think of how our lives will expand and deepen by means of his resurrection life!

Now that we have actually received this amazing friendship with God, we are no longer content to simply say it in plodding prose. We sing and shout our praises to God through Jesus, the Messiah!"

The total reality comes upon us so that we are in a continuing 'ANTICIPATED EXPECTATION' that our righteous relationship is secure, and we are overcomers 'In Him'.

It no longer is doom and gloom, so to speak but has become a life lived on that joyous relationship with Him through Jesus our Saviour and Lord.

James – the brother of Jesus – concerns himself with the fruitfulness of good works (he calls them charitable deeds) and speaks of such deeds occurring due to the faithful obedience of the believes and are the evidence of a genuine relationship with God based on Faith.

James 2:21-26; *"Wasn't our ancestor Abraham "made right with God by works" when he placed his son Isaac on the sacrificial altar? Isn't it obvious that faith and works are yoked partners, that faith expresses itself in works? That the works are "works of faith"?*

The full meaning of "believe" in the Scripture sentence, "Abraham believed God and was set right with God," includes his action. It's that mesh of believing and acting that got Abraham named "God's friend." Is it not evident that a person is made right with God not by a barren faith but by faith fruitful in works?

The same with Rahab, the Jericho harlot. Wasn't her action in hiding God's spies and helping them escape—that seamless unity of believing and doing—what counted with God? The very moment you separate body and spirit, you end up with a corpse. Separate faith and works and you get the same thing: a corpse." (See Joshua 2;)

Justification includes the assurance of salvation because Assurance is a subjective experience, an inner sureness resulting from the exercises of faith.

Justification is a judicial decree or declaration of God. Since God cannot lie, and He does not change, this judicial decision makes our restoration to His favour an objective and eternal reality.

Justification is the exact opposite of condemnation; it is God's acquittal. The God who has declared the case decided in our favour on the basis of the merits of Christ to whom we are joined by faith, and He will never again bring up the matter. For this reason, justification gives us peace with God, because it eliminates any legitimate source of condemnation. Paul writing to both the Christians in Rome and then again to the Christians in Ephesus is noticeably clear concerning the value of Justification being Gods' response to His Elect as against the 'natural condemnation' of the justice of the Law.

Romans 8:26-35; *"Meanwhile, the moment we get tired in the waiting, God's Spirit is right alongside helping us along. If we don't know how or what to pray, it doesn't matter. He does our praying in and for us, making prayer out of our wordless sighs, our aching groans. He knows us far better than we know ourselves, knows our pregnant condition, and keeps us present before God. That's why we can be so sure that every detail in our lives of love for God is worked into something good.*

God knew what he was doing from the very beginning. He decided from the outset to shape the lives of those who love him along the same lines as the life of his Son. The Son stands first in the line of humanity he restored. We see the original and intended shape of our lives there in him.

After God made that decision of what his children should be like, he followed it up by calling people by name. After he called them by name, he set them on a solid basis with himself. And then, after getting them established, he stayed with them to the end, gloriously completing what he had begun.

So, what do you think? With God on our side like this, how can we lose? If God didn't hesitate to put everything on the line for us, embracing our condition and exposing himself to the worst by sending his own Son. Is there anything else he wouldn't gladly and freely do for us?

And who would dare tangle with God by messing with one of God's chosen? Who would dare even to point a finger?

The One who died for us—who was raised to life for us! — is in the presence of God at this very moment sticking up for us.

Do you think anyone is going to be able to drive a wedge between us and Christ's love for us?

There is no way! Not trouble, not hard times, not hatred, not hunger, not homelessness, not bullying threats, not backstabbing, not even the worst sins listed in Scripture:"

Justification changes our position in relation to God. God no longer looks upon us apart from our union with Christ. Since He sees us "in Him" our acceptance is complete and final.

Romans 8:1; KJV. *"[There is] therefore now no condemnation to them which are in Christ Jesus, who walk not after the flesh, but after the Spirit."*

Ephesians 1:6; KJV. *"To the praise of the glory of his grace, wherein he has made us accepted in the beloved."*

Justification includes forgiveness of sins on the basis of the penalty already paid by Christ. God's wrath has already been fully placated (propitiated), and His holiness perfectly satisfied through Christ's self-sacrifice in payment for our sins (expiation).

* 'Christ Declared That His Work Was Finished; Therefore, God Continues To Consider It Finished.'

1 Thessalonians 5:9-11; *"God didn't set us up for an angry rejection but for salvation by our Master, Jesus Christ. He died for us, a death that triggered life. Whether we're awake with the living or asleep with the dead, we're alive with him!*

So, speak encouraging words to one another. Build up hope so you'll all be together in this, no one left out, no one left behind. I know you're already doing this; just keep on doing it."

Forgiveness is closely related to justification. God takes the initiative in forgiving us of all sin and iniquity, apart from anything we can do to merit His forgiveness. It is given freely as grace.

But like justification, forgiveness is only given to us in the form of pardon from penalty and release from guilt because sacrifice or atonement has already been paid.

Forgiveness does not mean, as so many seem to think, that penalty is set aside. To the contrary, in both the Old and New Testaments, forgiveness follows the payment of penalty as prescribed.

Leviticus 4:20; *"And he shall do with the bullock as he did with the bullock for a sin offering, so shall he do with this: and the priest shall make an atonement for them, and it shall be forgiven them."*

Matthew 26:26-28; *"During the meal, Jesus took and blessed the bread, broke it, and gave it to his disciples: Take, eat. This is my body.*

Taking the cup and thanking God, he gave it to them: Drink this, all of you. This is my blood, God's new covenant poured out for many people for the forgiveness of sins.

  The effectiveness of forgiveness differs in the Old and New Testaments for the simple reason that adequate payment or sacrifice to completely remove sin was not available until the offering of Christ Himself.

  Sins under the Old Covenant were forgiven and covered by the blood of animals offered as substitutionary sacrifices for the sinner who both confessed these sins and exercised faith in God's promise to forgive him.

  However, under the New Covenant, God is free to entirely separate the sinner from his sin, sending all remembrance of it away. Many times, the stronger term, "remission of sin" is translated from the same Greek word for forgiveness, "aphesis".

  By destroying all remembrance of sin, God can demonstrate His love and favour without restraint.

* 'God Guarantees Under The New Covenant To Forget Our Sins.
Because The Central Purpose Of God's Forgiveness Is To Restore His Fellowship With Man.'

Hebrews 8:10-13; *This new plan I'm making with Israel isn't going to be written on paper, isn't going to be chiselled in stone; This time I'm writing out the plan in them, carving it on the lining of their hearts. I'll be their God; they'll be my people.*

They won't go to school to learn about me, or buy a book called God in Five Easy Lessons. They'll all get to know me firsthand, the little and the big, the small and the great.

They'll get to know me by being kindly forgiven, with the slate of their sins forever wiped clean. By coming up with a new plan, a new covenant between God and his people, God put the old plan on the shelf. And there it stays, gathering dust. they'll be my people.

Acts 13:37-39; *"But the One God raised up—no dust and ashes for him! I want you to know, my very dear friends, that it is on account of this resurrected Jesus that the forgiveness of your sins can be promised.*

He accomplishes, in those who believe, everything that the Law of Moses could never make good on. But everyone who believes in this raised-up Jesus is declared good and right and whole before God."

God's decision to declare sinners righteous came from His own initiative. Nothing made Him do it. But from before the foundation of the earth – even before all men sinned – God planned a means of reconciliation through Christ.

* 'God Had Determined To Justify Man By Identifying Him With Jesus Christ.'

* 'By GRACE - unmerited favour. God's Riches At Christ's Expense.'

Romans 3:24; *"God did it for us. Out of sheer generosity he put us in right standing with himself. A pure gift. He got us out of the mess we're in and restored us to where he always wanted us to be. And he did it by means of Jesus Christ.*

By providing the REDEMPTION – the price – the blood of Christ.

Romans 5:6-11; *"Christ arrives right on time to make this happen. He didn't, and doesn't, wait for us to get ready. He presented himself for this sacrificial death when we were far too weak and rebellious to do anything to get ourselves ready. And even if we hadn't been so weak, we wouldn't have known what to do anyway.*

We can understand someone dying for a person worth dying for, and we can understand how someone good and noble could inspire us to selfless sacrifice. But God put his love on the line for us by offering his Son in sacrificial death while we were of no use whatever to him.

Now that we are set right with God by means of this sacrificial death, the consummate blood sacrifice, there is no longer a question of being at odds with God in any way. If, when we were at our worst, we were put on friendly terms with God by the sacrificial death of his Son, now that we're at our best, just think of how our lives will expand and deepen by means of his resurrection life!

Now that we have actually received this amazing friendship with God, we are no longer content to simply say it in plodding prose. We sing and shout our praises to God through Jesus, the Messiah!"

By the RESURRECTION – of Christ. The fresh start for a sinful people.

Romans 4:20-25; *"Abraham didn't tiptoe around God's promise asking cautiously sceptical questions. He plunged into the promise and came up strong, ready for God, sure that God would make good on what he had said. That's why it is said, "Abraham was declared fit before God by trusting God to set him right. But it's not just Abraham; it's also us!*

The same thing gets said about us when we embrace and believe the One who brought Jesus to life when the conditions were equally hopeless. The sacrificed Jesus made us fit for God, set us right with God."

By FAITH. We are justified in this New Life Reality.

Romans 5:1-2; *"By entering through faith into what God has always wanted to do for us—set us right with him, make us fit for him—we have it all together with God because of our Master Jesus.*

And that's not all: We throw open our doors to God and discover at the same moment that he has already thrown open his door to us. We find ourselves standing where we always hoped we might stand—out in the wide-open spaces of God's grace and glory, standing tall and shouting our praise."
By WORKS.

James 2:23-24; *"The full meaning of "believe" in the Scripture sentence, "Abraham believed God and was set right with God," includes his action. It's that mesh of believing and acting that got Abraham named "God's friend. "Is it not evident that a person is made right with God not by a barren faith but by faith fruitful in works?"*

Many are the times when the question as to whether, combinations of work and grace can be in harmony, so to speak. The answer is clearly presented in the above Scripture – *not by a barren faith but by faith fruitful in works?*

Grace by definition means "unmerited favour something we cannot earn or repay." There is nothing we can do or give to God to secure His favour. Certainly not in the sense of relying upon one or the other for salvation and God's favour. Instead, we must be receptive. As the result of grace working in us, changing our nature, we become able to do the good works God always purposed from before the beginning of the world.

But apart from redemption, we could not fulfil God's plans for us. All else are but dead works, and abominations in God's sight.

* 'Faith Is Simply Our Outstretched Hand To Receive All Grace Has To Give.'

Grace is not a reward for works.

Romans 4:4-5; *"If you're a hard worker and do a good job, you deserve your pay; we don't call your wages a gift. But if you see that the job is too big for you, that it's something only God can do, and you trust him to do it—you could never do it for yourself no matter how hard and long you worked—well, that trusting-him-to-do-it is what gets you set right with God, by God. Sheer gift."*

The common-sense – the logical – understanding would be that from God's perspective, He does not owe us anything at all.

It is we who receive all that He has to give us. Therefore, He is the giver of gifts even when we are the receiver of wages for the work we have done.

Reliance upon works nullifies grace.

Romans 11:5-6; *"It's the same today. There's a fiercely loyal minority still—not many, perhaps, but probably more than you think. They're holding on, not because of what they think they're going to get out of it, but because they're convinced of God's grace and purpose in choosing them. If they were only thinking of their own immediate self-interest, they would have left long ago."*

In summary then, it is not by our works that we have a right-standing – Righteousness – with God but, it is by our personal faith, that we enter into such relationship, and that is because of what Christ Jesus did for us at Calvary.

* 'Salvation by faith in grace expresses itself in good works.'

Philippians 2:12-16; *"What I'm getting at, friends, is that you should simply keep on doing what you've done from the beginning. When I was living among you, you lived in responsive obedience. Now that I'm separated from you, keep it up. Better yet, redouble your efforts.*

Be energetic in your life of salvation, reverent and sensitive before God. That energy is God's energy, an energy deep within you, God himself willing and working at what will give him the most pleasure. Do everything readily and cheerfully—no bickering, no second-guessing allowed!

Go out into the world uncorrupted, a breath of fresh air in this squalid and polluted society. Provide people with a glimpse of good living and of the living God.
Carry the light-giving Message into the night so I'll have good cause to be proud of you on the day that Christ

returns. You'll be living proof that I didn't go to all this work for nothing."

* 'A Part Of The New Creation Is Being Made Able To Fulfil God's Will.'

Ephesians 2:10; KJV. *"For we are his workmanship, created in Christ Jesus unto good works, which God has before ordained that we should walk in them."*

The challenging question is this: Is the law of Moses applicable to believers today?

This is still the question which is relevant to the people of this current generation as it was in the days of Jesus and the apostles all those years ago. And a vital truth in this time is that the Christian believer has to be able to answer this question not from the Scriptures alone, but it must be answered by the testimony of the believer as the witness of the truth within their own living.

It becomes an imperative for the witness to be very personal, rather than doctrinal in response and must be evidenced in the manner of their own living.

The Jews were constantly insisting that Christians submit to the ordinances of the Jewish law in order to be saved. This included not only observing the Sabbath, but also physical circumcision and dietary restrictions.

However, in this the dispensation of Grace discussed earlier, in Christ these requirements are all done away with, and all reliance is put upon Him as the one and only way for the sinner to be set free and the act of salvation to be completed IN HIM. – that is – to be saved.

Although historically this question was settled at the Council of Jerusalem once and for all. I believe that it still needs, that clarification – through the personal testimony of the believer – to be effective.

Even in those early days of the New Testament after Paul and Barnabas had evidenced notable success, preaching among the Gentiles, certain leaders became concerned that these Gentile converts conform to the law of Moses.

Controversy continued until the apostles all met together, when James became the spokesman voicing the direction of God when he said:

Acts 15:19-29; *"So here is my decision: We're not going to unnecessarily burden non-Jewish people who turn to the Master. We'll write them a letter and tell them,*
'Be careful to not get involved in activities connected with idols, to guard the morality of sex and marriage, to not serve food offensive to Jewish Christians—blood, for instance.'

This is basic wisdom from Moses, preached and honoured for centuries now in city after city as we have met and kept the Sabbath."

What a wonderful thing it is for us in this present time to see that the pattern of the Old Testament days of

Moses is just as well practiced today as it was throughout the period of the early Christian church. It acknowledges the Grace elements associated within the God and His people throughout all of HIStory.

The question therefore is for us quite simple does Law – override – Grace? As Paul is won't to say GOD FORBID.

Everyone agreed: apostles, leaders, all the people. They picked Judas – not Iscariot – but he *(nicknamed Barsabbas) and Silas—they both carried considerable weight in the church—and sent them to Antioch with Paul and Barnabas with this letter: 'From the apostles and leaders, your friends, to our friends in Antioch, Syria, and Cilicia: Hello! We heard that some men from our church went to you and said things that confused and upset you. Mind you, they had no authority from us; we didn't send them. We have agreed unanimously to pick representatives and send them to you with our good friends Barnabas and Paul.*

We picked men we knew you could trust, Judas and Silas— they've looked death in the face time and again for the sake of our Master Jesus Christ. We've sent them to confirm in a face-to-face meeting with you what we've written. It seemed to the Holy Spirit and to us that you should not be saddled with any crushing burden but be responsible only for these bare necessities.

Be careful not to get involved in activities connected with idols; avoid serving food offensive to Jewish Christians (blood, for instance); and guard the morality of sex and marriage. These guidelines are sufficient to keep relations congenial between us. And God be with you!"

The law is a whole system in itself. Those who keep the law place themselves under a curse if they fail to keep all of it. We cannot decide to do some of the commandments and neglect others. The blessings and the curses of the law equally depended on submission to the total – all of it – contained in the Mosaic covenant.

Galatians 3:10; *"For as many as are of the works of the law are under the curse: for it is written, Cursed [is] every one that continues not in all things which are written in the book of the law to do them."*

We all – without exception – fall from grace when we attempt to follow both the law and the gospel. Most often the urge to add works to grace comes from an inadequate trust, not only in self, but also a lack of assurance, caused in the main by poor teaching of God's Word.

> * 'God Will Tolerate No Mixtures.
> It Is Either Grace Or Law.
> You Can Add Nothing To Grace.'

Jesus clearly defined the works of God as believing – relying – upon Him.

John 6:28-29; *"Then said they unto him, What shall we do, that we might work the works of God? Jesus answered and said unto them, This is the work of God, that you believe on him whom he has sent."*

Faith works by a love that only God can give to us. The law is summarized in the one word "love." Some of the Church Fathers sought to make love the work that justified, but this cannot be the gracious working of the Holy Spirit within him.

* 'Love Is A Fruit Of Our Union With God.
It Is An Outworking Of The New Relationship
And We Enter Into That Relationship By Faith.'

Galatians 5:4-6; *"I suspect you would never intend this, but this is what happens. When you attempt to live by your own religious plans and projects, you are cut off from Christ, you fall out of grace.*

Meanwhile we expectantly wait for a satisfying relationship with the Spirit. For in Christ, neither our most conscientious religion nor disregard of religion amounts to anything. What matters is something far more interior: faith expressed in love."

For me personally this was just the message I needed, and it came at the most crucial time in my life.

I had only seen God as a religious figure way beyond my limited understanding and knowledge. A frightening – almost despairing – factor for me to deal with. So, I had stopped even wanting to know more about this un-obtainable entity. It was at such a time as this, that

I, through a series of, for me, unrelated circumstances, met a real Christian Family.

I found a profound relationship within that family setting, and for the first time in my until then – 36 years of living – I knew what was missing in my life.

Relationship with Jesus was beyond the Law and beyond Knowledge, but it was all to do with something called Faith. Not long after I said to YES to Jesus and became His disciple, I coined a phrase that I soon realised came from the Holy Spirit:

* 'Christian Hope Is An Anticipated Expectation, and Is The Reality Of God's Way Not Mine.'

Romans 5:1-5; *"By entering through faith into what God has always wanted to do for us—set us right with him, make us fit for him—we have it all together with God because of our Master Jesus. And that's not all: We throw open our doors to God and discover at the same moment that he has already thrown open his door to us. We find ourselves standing where we always hoped we might stand—out in the wide-open spaces of God's grace and glory, standing tall and shouting our praise.*

There's more to come: We continue to shout our praise even when we're hemmed in with troubles, because we know how troubles can develop passionate patience in us, and how that patience in turn forges the tempered steel of virtue, keeping us alert for whatever God will do next.

In alert expectancy such as this, we're never left feeling short-changed. Quite the contrary—we can't round up enough containers to hold everything God generously pours into our lives through the Holy Spirit!"

Chapter Nine.
"REDEMPTION THROUGH FAITH IN HIS BLOOD."

Ephesians 1:5-14; *"Having predestined us unto the adoption of children by Jesus Christ to himself, according to the good pleasure of his will, To the praise of the glory of his grace, wherein he hath made us accepted in the beloved. In whom we have redemption through his blood, the forgiveness of sins, according to the riches of his grace;*

Wherein he hath abounded toward us in all wisdom and prudence; Having made known unto us the mystery of his will, according to his good pleasure which he has purposed in himself: That in the dispensation of the fulness of times he might gather together in one all things in Christ, both which are in heaven, and which are on earth; [even] in him: In whom also we have obtained an inheritance, being predestined according to the purpose of him who works all things after the counsel of his own will:

That we should be to the praise of his glory, who first trusted in Christ. In whom you also [trusted], after that you heard the word of truth, the gospel of your salvation: in whom also after that you believed, you were sealed with that holy Spirit of promise,
Which is the earnest of our inheritance until the redemption of the purchased possession, unto the praise of his glory."

Psalm 49:7-8; *"None [of them] can by any means redeem his brother, nor give to God a ransom for him: (For the redemption of their soul [is] precious, and it is ceased for ever:)"*

Redemption is the effective power of salvation resulting from our faith toward God, whilst Justification is a legal decree of acquittal from guilt and penalty. Redemption is therefore the actual transaction resulting in our deliverance from sin. "Webster lists four meanings which apply to the theological use of the verb "to redeem" and I list them here so that we all may gain the context upheld in Scripture:

1. to buy back or repurchase; to regain title by purchase;

2. to liberate from slavery or captivity by paying a price;

3. to release from alien claims or clear from debt;

4. to repossess upon fulfilment of an obligation;

Redemption is always the payment of a set price or ransom to secure the release of one in debt, bondage, or slavery. So, from the time of Adam and Eve being the first sinners, so to speak, all mankind has come bondage to Satan, and the price being so exceedingly high, have sold their respective freedom into the slavery of sin.

We lost, not only our covenant inheritance, but our personal freedom. Remember that we are unable to redeem ourselves but needed someone from outside to come and pay the price of his release. Christ gave Himself as our ransom.

Mark 10:45; *"For even the Son of man came not to be ministered unto, but to minister, and to give his life a ransom for many."*

Only because the blood of Jesus Christ fully satisfies the demands of God's justice, is He free to declare us righteous.

When we look at this satisfaction from a priestly standpoint, we are dealing with the idea of atonement. But when we look at this same satisfaction in terms of a payment or a price to repurchase a lost possession, we are dealing with the idea of redemption. In either case, it is the blood of Jesus Christ which met all demands for payment.

Roman 3:24-25; *"Being justified freely by his grace through the redemption that is in Christ Jesus: Whom God had set forth [to be] a propitiation through faith in his blood, to declare his righteousness for the remission of sins that are past, through the forbearance of God;"*

God never intended for His people to continue as slaves under foreign dominion, or to lose their family inheritance through poverty and indebtedness. He made provision for regaining personal possessions and maintaining family honour.

Redemption is the personal intervention of the nearest of kin to restore persons or property to those with a rightful interest in them. Christ became man and our elder brother in order to be our nearest of kin.

Galatians 4:4-5; *"But when the fulness of the time was come, God sent forth his Son, made of a woman, made under the law, To redeem them that were under the law, that we might receive the adoption of sons."*

Redemption is the exercise of power in giving effect deliverance from the penalty of sin. When those who hold God's people do so unlawfully, God may not pay a price to redeem them. Instead, He may exercise His Almighty power and bring them out of bondage and captivity by His outstretched hand. The exodus from Egypt is a beautiful picture of our deliverance from the power of darkness.

Exodus 14:30; *"Thus the LORD saved Israel that day out of the hand of the Egyptians; and Israel saw the Egyptians dead upon the sea shore."*

The Old Testament specifies rights of redemption to the nearest of kin regarding both close relatives and property. These rights were carried out when Boaz took Ruth as his wife and thereby restored the family inheritance and preserved the honour of the family name. This and the many other examples of redemption rights in the Old Testament were types picturing the "rightness" of God's repossession of His people through the blood of Christ.

The kinsman-redeemer had several specific rights under the law. Everyone had to respect his rights. He could either exercise them or neglect them as he chose. He had therefore the following options:

1. To purchase back a forfeited inheritance:

Leviticus 25:23-28; *"The land shall not be sold for ever: for the land [is] mine; for you [are] strangers and sojourners with me. And in all the land of your possession you shall grant a redemption for the land. If your brother be waxen poor and has sold away [some] of his possession, and if any of his kin come to redeem it, then shall he redeem that which his brother sold.*
And if the man has none to redeem it, and himself be able to redeem it; Then let him count the years of the sale thereof and restore the overplus unto the man to whom he sold it; that he may return unto his possession. But if he be not able to restore [it] to him, then that which is sold shall remain in the hand of him that had bought it until the year of jubilee: and in the jubilee it shall go out, and he shall return unto his possession."

    * 'Christ Brought Us Back, But He Also Restored Our Right To Share An Inheritance In God.
He Not Only Set Us Free, But Made Us Heirs, Joint Heirs, With Himself.'

2. To ransom his kinsman from bondage to a foreigner:

Leviticus 25:47-49; *"And if a sojourner or stranger wax rich because of your efforts, and your brother [that dwells] by him wax poor, and sell himself unto the stranger [or] sojourner by you, or to the stock of the stranger's family:*

After that he is sold, he may be redeemed again; one of his brethren may redeem him:"

Sin is a thought or action – usually of a brief or temporary nature - that is seen as a drop – change – in behaviour and is foreign to the living standards of Godly people. We were not designed to be enslaved to sin, because Christ gave Himself to pay the price according to God's justice; but He went even further in that He, Christ, effectively destroyed the power of sin over us.

3. To avenge the death of a slain kinsman, to maintain family honour:

Numbers 5:8; *"But if the man have no kinsman to recompense the trespass unto, let the trespass be recompensed unto the LORD, [even] to the priest; beside the ram of the atonement, whereby an atonement shall be made for him."*

Numbers 35:12; *"And they shall be unto you cities for refuge from the avenger; that the manslayer die not, until he stands before the congregation in judgment."*

Deuteronomy 19:6; *"Lest the avenger of the blood pursue the slayer, while his heart is hot, and overtake him, because the way is long, and slay him; whereas he [was] not worthy of death, inasmuch as he hated him not in time past."*

We were dead in our trespasses and sins; but God had always purposed that we should be His children, members of His family and household. He defeated the Murderer – that is Satan – and made us alive again together with Him.

4. To marry the widow of the deceased kinsman:

Ruth 3:7-18; *"Boaz had a good time, eating and drinking his fill—he felt great. Then he went off to get some sleep, lying down at the end of a stack of barley. Ruth quietly followed; she lay down to signal her availability for marriage.*

In the middle of the night the man was suddenly startled and sat up. Surprise! This woman asleep at his feet! He said, "And who are you?" She said, "I am Ruth, your maiden; take me under your protecting wing. You're my close relative, you know, in the circle of covenant redeemers—you do have the right to marry me." He said, "GOD bless you, my dear daughter! What a splendid expression of love! And when you could have had your pick of any of the young men around. And now, my dear daughter, don't you worry about a thing; I'll do all you could want or ask. Everybody in town knows what a courageous woman you are—a real prize! You're right, I am a close relative to you, but there is one even closer than I am. So, stay the rest of the night. In the morning, if he wants to exercise his customary rights and responsibilities as the closest covenant redeemer, he'll have his chance; but if he isn't interested, as GOD lives, I'll do it.

Now go back to sleep until morning." Ruth slept at his feet until dawn, but she got up while it was still dark and wouldn't be recognized.

Then Boaz said to himself, "No one must know that Ruth came to the threshing floor." So, Boaz said, "Bring the shawl you're wearing and spread it out." She spread it out and he poured it full of barley, six measures, and put it on her shoulders. Then she went back to town. When she came to her mother-in-law, Naomi asked, "And how did things go, my dear daughter?" Ruth told her everything that the man had done for her, adding, "And he gave me all this barley besides—six quarts! He told me, 'You can't go back empty-handed to your mother-in-law!' Naomi said, "Sit back and relax, my dear daughter, until we find out how things turn out; that man isn't going to fool around. Mark my words, he's going to get everything wrapped up today."

Ruth 4:1-13; *"Boaz went straight to the public square and took his place there. Before long, the "closer relative," the one mentioned earlier by Boaz, strolled by. "Step aside, old friend," said Boaz. "Take a seat." The man sat down. Boaz then gathered ten of the town elders together and said.*

"Sit down here with us; we've got some business to take care of." And they sat down.
Boaz then said to his relative, "The piece of property that belonged to our relative Elimelech is being sold by his widow Naomi, who has just returned from the country of Moab. I thought you ought to know about it. Buy it back if you want it—you can make it official in the presence of

those sitting here and before the town elders. You have first redeemer rights. If you don't want it, tell me so I'll know where I stand. You're first in line to do this and I'm next after you." He said, "I'll buy it."

Then Boaz added, "You realize, don't you, that when you buy the field from Naomi, you also get Ruth the Moabite, the widow of our dead relative, along with the redeemer responsibility to have children with her to carry on the family inheritance." Then the relative said, "Oh, I can't do that—I'd jeopardize my own family's inheritance. You go ahead and buy it—you can have my rights—I can't do it."

In the olden times in Israel, this is how they handled official business regarding matters of property and inheritance: a man would take off his shoe and give it to the other person. This was the same as an official seal or personal signature in Israel. So, when Boaz's "redeemer" relative said, "Go ahead and buy it," he signed the deal by pulling off his shoe.

Boaz then addressed the elders and all the people in the town square that day: "You are witnesses today that I have bought from Naomi everything that belonged to Elimelech and Killion and Mahlon, including responsibility for Ruth the foreigner, the widow of Mahlon—I'll take her as my wife and keep the name of the deceased alive along with his inheritance. The memory and reputation of the deceased is not going to disappear out of this family or from his hometown. To all this you are witnesses this very day."

All the people in the town square that day, backing up the elders, said, "Yes, we are witnesses. May GOD make this woman who is coming into your household like Rachel and Leah, the two women who built the family of Israel. May GOD make you a pillar in Ephrathah and famous in Bethlehem! With the children GOD gives you from this young woman, may your family rival the family of Perez, the son Tamar bore to Judah." Boaz married Ruth. She became his wife. Boaz slept with her. By GOD's gracious gift she conceived and had a son.

I do not apologise for the length of the above Scripture referring to this story from the Old Testament days, because I believe that it gives a salient perspective to the present-day overseers in Christian fellowships. It is precisely because they have become the 'caretakers' – overseers of the collective Bride of Christ – with all the responsibilities and accountabilities – that such were the obligations expected through the redeemer-ship given and accepted by Boaz.

Therefore, I respectfully submit that it is the same – in this dispensation 2023 – to those of us who are the overseers of the Christian church until the coming of the King of Kings P.T.L.

However, I wish to point out that because we no longer are a people under 'Law' but are, because of Christ, living in the dispensation of Grace, those in oversight are the true Christian Overseers caring for the members spiritual welfare, rather than the Humanistic caretaker mode which by definition is in a care-taking mode and with respect are considered as taking rather than giving responsibility to those for whom they have charge.

The ministers of the congregation in this 21st century are leaders not dictators, and should attend their congregants in leading them by personal example, not by dictate.

Acts 20:28; *"Now it's up to you. Be on your toes—both for yourselves and your congregation of sheep. The Holy Spirit has put you in charge of these people—God's people they are—to guard and protect them. God himself thought they were worth dying for."*

* 'Christ Not Only Bought The Church With His Own Blood But Made Her His Bride.'

Redemption is the full recovery of God's people; a complete restoration to His possession. Deliverance in Christ is total and complete: To make this possible, Christ strips every competing claim from power and cancels every legal debt.

Christ redeemed us from sin.

Psalm 130:7-8; *"Let Israel hope in the LORD: for with the LORD [there is] mercy, and with him [is] plenteous redemption. And he shall redeem Israel from all his iniquities."*

Christ redeemed us from the law and its curses.

Galatians 3:13-14; *"Christ has redeemed us from the curse of the law, being made a curse for us: for it is written, Cursed [is] every one that hangs on a tree: That the blessing of Abraham might come on the Gentiles through Jesus Christ; that we might receive the promise of the Spirit through faith."*

Christ redeemed us from death.

Hosea 13:14; *"I will ransom them from the power of the grave; I will redeem them from death: O death, I will be your plagues; O grave, I will be your destruction: repentance shall be hid from mine eyes."*

The question I had when I began my New Life in Christ – and I am sure that I will never be a lone voice with this question – is simply put:

How does redemption result in change within my life?

Redemption, already a reality to those who believe, only becomes real to us as we take hold of its reward and that can only be gained by our individual Faith. This is the example of faith towards God, that He, Who through His Son Jesus paid the only – absolute – price proscribed as appropriate under the law.

As we agree with God that the blood of Jesus was a sufficient price to purchase us, we begin to enjoy the liberty He purchased for us as children of God.

But liberty, even when it is real and objective, is not enjoyed until it is accepted as fact and acted upon.

We have many stories on record of liberated slaves or prisoners of war who remained in their sad condition because freedom seemed too good to be true.

The truth dawned for me, that moment in time, when the Light of the Gospel was revealed to me, it was that moment when 'I let go and let God', so to speak. When my spiritual eyes were finally opened and reality became my everlasting truth, I embraced the gospel – or good news – by faith.

Then and only then did I experience my freedom or redemption in practical ways which not only could I understand but could put into place – sometimes stumbling – as the Holy Spirit directed:

Titus 2:14; *"Who gave himself for us, that he might redeem us from all iniquity, and purify unto himself a peculiar people, zealous of good works."*

The term "peculiar" here means "of great value." It comes from one of the ancient practices of valuing things. God had made us a people of His own possession, and we are therefore valued in and through the blood of Christ! So, when we become caught up in our old selves and such patterns of behaviour that are contrary to the will purposed by our redeemer Christ we stray away from our enthused relationship with God – also with our fellow beings here on earth – and slip down in our own worthiness and sluggish behaviours, forgetting that the fact of our deliverance from such attitudes has already been paid.

We just need to realize that we are delivered and free from our past unto our new reality in Christ Jesus, a Spontaneous and Joyful return to God.

Isaiah 44:22-23; *"I have blotted out, as a thick cloud, your transgressions, and, as a cloud, your sins: return unto me; for I have redeemed you.*

Sing, O you heavens; for the LORD has done [it]: shout, you lower parts of the earth: break forth into singing, you mountains, O forest, and every tree therein: for the LORD has redeemed Jacob and glorified himself in Israel."

Many times, our spontaneity and joy in the Lord are stifled because we allow doubt and condemnation to put a wet blanket, so to speak, over our faith.

John 10:10; *"The thief has come to kill, steal and destroy But I am come that you should have life abundantly."*

Satan is the deceiver and God in Christ is the redeemer and therefore our sins and the remembrance of such as was our old life has not only been accounted but also redeemed thus taken off of the ledger of our debt and never more to be held to our account. We must therefore forget them too, as a discipline of faith.

We will look forward to times of fellowship with God when guilt is not nagging inside.

Colossians 1:13-14; *"Who has delivered us from the power of darkness, and has translated [us] into the kingdom of his dear Son: In whom we have redemption through his blood, [even] the forgiveness of sins:"*

Through redemption Deliverance has already been purchased and become ours when we receive the faith to accept it. It is then that we can stand in our right of freedom. We can have the power of habit broken through the authority of the name of Jesus.

When I was young and believed that I was an orphan due to circumstances arising from the Blitz in London during the 2nd World War, I developed a sense of loneliness – of not knowing who I was, or who I belonged too.

This became more of a depressing nature when I discovered as a teenager that I had no ability to relate to a meaningful relationship connecting my past – of which I had none – to the future expectations, which were pessimistic due to my inability to read or write properly, thus gave little chance – because of such a mindset – to hope of the future.

In hindsight – what a wonderful addition to the English vocabulary – I can see many incidences when something – some force, I now know to have been the – Holy Spirit of God – spoke and or guided me away from danger.

Now I can believe it was the Spirit of God Who had me in His care, but in those days, I had no knowledge of such things. Then in the mid-1970's, I had an encounter that changed my mind-set for ever, I met Jesus. (The story is written in the following chapter 10.)

A deepening knowledge of belonging to God became not only a quest, but also became my passion. For it has been in such a pursuit I began to know who I was and with whom I am related.

1 Corinthians 6:19-20; *"What? know you not that your body is the temple of the Holy Ghost [which is] in you, which you have of God, and you are not your own? For you are bought with a price: therefore, glorify God in your body, and in your spirit, which are God's."*

The truth is that we are redeemed – purchased – so that we become God's property. He has the right to decide what to do with us. This means we must use our bodies, our personalities, and spirits as He desires. Not until we realize the fact that we are God's possession and that He comes into us to live, do we have the motivation we need to live holy lives and to take care of our bodies and minds.

Another of those favourite chorus which I still sing today is:

It's no longer I that live, but Christ that lives in me.
It's no longer I that live but Christ that lives in me.
He lives, He lives Jesus is alive in me.
It's no longer I that live, but Christ that lives in me.
S. Ellis: from Galatians 2:20:

* 'We No Longer Belong To Nobody, Even Ourselves, But We Belong To God.'

However, it is an imperative that we the believer must come to the reality that our experience of redemption never complete in the sense that there is a long journey, which I like to term as lifelong.

For example, such as salvation is a combination of past, present, and future, in all its applications.

Therefore, Redemption is no exception. While we have already received forgiveness of sins and are presently finding release from the power of sin, we have yet to receive complete removal of the presence of sin – that which is termed as "the redemption of our body."?

Scripture tells us quite clearly that the redemption of our body does not take place until Christ's return.

Romans 8:23; *"And not only [they], but ourselves also, which have the first fruits of the Spirit, even we ourselves groan within ourselves, waiting for the adoption, [to wit], the redemption of our body."*

We hope – with that 'Anticipated Expectation' – and wait for this because it is embedded into the future of Christ's soon return and that has not happened yet.

Romans 8:24-25; *"For we are saved by hope: but hope that is seen is not hope: for what a man sees, why does he yet hope for? But if we hope for that we see not, [then] do we with patience wait for [it]."*

Upon Christ's return – at the Second Coming – we will all be gathered before the Lord in heaven to sing His praise.

Revelation 5:9; *"And they sung a new song, saying, Thou are worthy to take the book, and to open the seals thereof: for you were slain, and have redeemed us to God by your blood out of every kindred, and tongue, and people, and nation;"*

When that time comes, we will be completely separated from the world.

Exodus 8:23; *"And I will put a division between my people and your people: tomorrow shall this sign be."*

Let me explain just one of the Hebrew words for redemption (p"dooth). The above Scripture was attributed as quoted by Moses to Pharoah, before the plague of flies began.

God sent flies to overrun Egypt, but Goshen the suburb in which his, that is God's, people lived, was free from the plague of flies and also the other plagues sent to the Egyptians of that time. This is an illustration, if you will, of God differencing between those who are His of the promise, and those who are not.

God in and through redemption makes the difference in lives not only then but also today and the future. between those who were His and those who were not. He will do this again at His return. He has promised to take those whom He has redeemed, His people, away with him.

Chapter Ten:

'NOW'
THE ONLY TIME WE HAVE WITH JESUS."

There are many questions to be answered in regard to the Scripture found in Paul's letter to the Roman believers and I can only give you my understanding which satisfied me personally. In this respect I will endeavour from my memory and notations from my early Christian walk, to answer of some of those biblical questions.

Romans 10:12-21; NKJV. *"For there is no distinction between Jew and Greek, for the same Lord over all is rich to all who call upon Him. For "whoever calls on the name of the LORD shall be saved."*

Our personal response to God's Righteousness is never achieved by our works but by our hearts – read spiritual – response to His Holy Word. This is always available to us because we are made in His image and likeness, which in its wholeness means that we are always related to Him through His Word.

How then shall they call on Him in whom they have not believed?

There is a marked contrast between believing and knowing something.

For me it was the evidence and witness of the one who spoke to me concerning Jesus – it was a believing through the trust I had in the one who was speaking and how I perceived their integrity and sincerity in sharing their personal belief with me. But it is also because there has always been a quest in me to find a real place of belonging. For those of you who have not read my earlier works let me just explain.

I was invited to have dinner with a Christian family in Moe and saw in that family a picture of what I had perhaps dreamed of throughout my first thirty-five years of life.

I saw and experienced a love in operation – Dad and Mum with five children which had an obvious healthy relationship one with the other. This picture then became a reality which transcended anything I had known before. To cut a long story, at the end of a wonderful evening I sat in my car and reflected, that what this family had, was what I desired for my life and the living of it.

No Bible bashing was required, no reprimand of my many failings over the years, but an evidence of what was possible and was within me; a burning desire.

And how shall they believe in Him of whom they have not heard?

Some weeks later I received an invitation to hear a speaker who was a Chaplain at a major prison in the Asian region. A private dinner would be before the meeting and that was also a part of the invitation.
The visiting Chaplain was 'Mumma Olga' who was the female Chaplain at an all-male prison, and was someone

with whom I could relate, in that I was at that time a Probation and Parole Officer in Victoria. This together with my past experiences, made me very attentive to what she had to say.

She spoke to a packed meeting about how Jesus was not only her inspiration but also her strength throughout her career. I wrote down many things, but one stood out from my notes, and it was that her employment was, for her, not a Job, but a 'calling' She said that she would not be able to do the work without God's help and the empowerment of the Holy Spirit.

Now, remember, that I had never heard of the Holy Spirit as a separate entity. She explained that without the Holy Spirit being her guide she would not be effective.

The Chaplain continued to speak as if this Holy Spirit was very personal to her, and this is what drew me to continue to think upon these new factors in relationships over the following coming weeks.

And how shall they hear without a preacher?

Some weeks went by, and I was returning from refereeing a soccer match in a town some good distance – 100klm – from my home. It was a very cold and wet Sunday afternoon and there were no change facilities to get cleaned up or even dried after the game. I was on my way home when I distinctly heard a voice speaking to me.

Now apart from me and my dog, a Pyrenean Mountain Dog, there was no living thing in my car, and remember that the Dog was of French dissent and therefore, did not speak English – now I know that I have never been good at telling jokes O.K. – so in a state of shock, I stopped the car and reflected upon those words that I had heard. The voice just said that I was to go to that particular church for the evening meeting and that he – God – would meet me there.

Again, to cut the story short I went to the meeting arriving just a few minutes late and longing to not be noticed, I looked for a seat at the rear of the church just in case I wanted to leave early.

The preacher was Ps. Bruce Gilding, the assistant Pastor of the Church, and I continue to regard him very highly through the many years since that night. I discovered that the message was the answer to my question arising from the previous meeting with the visiting Chaplain a few weeks prior.

The preacher was undoubtably answering my concerns about who was the Holy Spirit. I had heard God speak to me in the car and I heard Him again speak to me at that meeting, and when the invitation was given at the conclusion of his preaching I responded and have never had a moment of regret since that wonderful release.

And how shall they preach unless they are sent? "How beautiful are the feet of those who preach the gospel of peace, Who bring glad tidings of good things!"

Much 'Living Water' has come into my life since those early New Life experiences, and many changes have occurred. I thank God for the consistency of the Word in my life which has been both my guide and my fortress.

However, it was impressed incredibly early that we all have a 'Calling' and so it has been the evidence of such a calling that has enabled me to preach in many places in Australia, as well as in India and for the past seventeen years in the wonderful country of Sri Lanka.

I thank God that just as He spoke to me in that car, He has been a constant part of my life ever since, He knows best, and just like a car, I need to have a grease and oil change – as a regular rejuvenation check – That's where the Holy Spirit becomes my regular companion – to keep me in tune with God's perfect will and calling upon my life.

But they have not all obeyed the gospel. For Isaiah says, "Lord, who has believed our report?"

A fundamental premise of Christianity is that God sends His Word, but humankind is not compelled to either believe or accept it. It has always been in front of humankind and God is keen for mankind – which He created – to accept it, so that the broken relationship, of equal trust, can be restored.

So then, faith comes by hearing, and hearing by the word of God.

When I accepted Jesus as my Saviour and Lord, I was determined to learn as much as I could about the maintenance of my Salvation. I saw at the very beginning that my faith will always be strengthened by my understanding of my relationship status with God my Creator. And that can, most profitably be through my personal investment and understanding in His Word.

But I say, have they not heard? Yes indeed: "Their sound has gone out to all the earth, And their words to the ends of the world."

Paul is addressing the Jews living in Rome but the reference to the Gentiles is a direct application to those of the peoples of the earth in this modern time 2024 A.D.

When see the overall reach of God's Word and in particular, His Divine Principles within the last two thousand years, and where the Gospel has been proclaimed by faithful messengers in almost all countries and populations of the world. That same message, of that same 'Good News' that Jesus is way and the truth and therefore the Life for all who would seek him.

We know that Yes is the answer. But remember that although the Word has been proclaimed the hearer may be persuaded to accept or reject the invitation to respond in a positive or negative manner. It is, as it always has been, a choice of the free will of the hearer.

* 'Yes, To God's Way Means No To Satan, I Choose God's Way. Do You?'

But I say, did Israel not know? First Moses says: "I will provoke you to jealousy by those who are not a nation, I will move you to anger by a foolish nation." But Isaiah is very bold and says: "I was found by those who did not seek Me; I was made manifest to those who did not ask for Me." But to Israel he says: "All day long I have stretched out My hands To a disobedient and contrary people."

The time is closing in upon us all, we don't, in a normal sense, decide the time and circumstances of our death.

But this I do know, God has purposed that none of us will have foreknowledge of such things, but He is coming soon, we live in the certainty that there will be no time to change our ways at that time, and such certainty confirms:

BUT THE 'NOW TIME' IS ALL WE HAVE:

1 Peter 1:3-9; *"What a God we have! And how fortunate we are to have him, this Father of our Master Jesus! Because Jesus was raised from the dead, we've been given a brand-new life and have everything to live for, including a future in heaven—and the future starts now!*
God is keeping careful watch over us and the future. The Day is coming when you'll have it all—life healed and whole. I know how great this makes you feel, even though you have to put up with every kind of aggravation in the meantime. Pure gold put in the fire comes out of it proved pure; genuine faith put through this suffering comes out

proved genuine. When Jesus wraps this all up, it's your faith, not your gold, that God will have on display as evidence of his victory.

You never saw him, yet you love him. You still don't see him, yet you trust him—with laughter and singing. Because you kept on believing, you'll get what you're looking forward to: total salvation."

A mantra that is often used to stir people is *'The just shall live by faith'*, but alas it is not so easily understood without spiritual input.

This statement occurs four times in the King James Version. In each context more meaning is added to it. Basically, it means that we not only begin our walk with God by exercising faith toward God, but we continue walking with him in the same way.

Once the foundation has been laid, faith becomes our new principle of life.

The basic attitude of faith is one of trust and is able to be received with the new ideas and concepts. We continue to receive from God this way when our relationship with Him is restored to the level it was between God and Adam in the Eden at the beginning, so to speak.

* 'Faith, Like Repentance, Is Something We Will Go On Using The Rest Of Our Lives.'

Colossians 2:6-7; *"As you have therefore received Christ Jesus the Lord, [so] walk in him: Rooted and built up in him, and stablished in the faith, as you have been taught, abounding therein with thanksgiving."*

Living by faith means living expectantly toward God. We have not received all of God's promises yet, but what we have received should strengthen our hope and anticipation for what is to come. What God has promised all of us, as His children, and what He has spoken to us individually, will surely come to pass if we wait for it. It means actively adhering to the promises, giving ourselves to them, and allowing them to shape our expectation. Waiting means more than allowing time to pass; In the context of Faith waiting has the same foundation as does the word Hope: 'An Anticipated Expectation.'

Habakkuk 2:3-4; *"For the vision [is] yet for an appointed time, but at the end it shall speak, and not lie: though it tarry, wait for it; because it will surely come, it will not tarry. Behold, his soul [which] is lifted up is not upright in him: but the just shall live by his faith."*

Living by faith means growing in reliance on God as knowledge of Him increases. The more revelation of God we receive through His Word, the more we have to lean upon or trust. Each time we experience the faithfulness of God to His promises, the easier it becomes to anticipate that He will fulfil the other things He has said He will do for us.

The truth concerning Faith, is that, of itself it produces faith, and the Gospel – Good News – plays no favourites.

Romans 1:16-17; *"For I am not ashamed of the gospel of Christ: for it is the power of God unto salvation to everyone that believes; to the Jew first, and also to the Greek. For therein is the righteousness of God revealed from faith to faith: as it is written, The just shall live by faith."*

Living by faith means release from all self-effort. We no longer attempt to add anything to the merits of the blood of Jesus Christ.

We allow the blood to speak peace within and are not tricked into some subtle means of trying to earn God's grace.

Galatians 3:11-13; *"But that no man is justified by the law in the sight of God, [it is] evident: for, The just shall live by faith. And the law is not of faith: but the man that is bound up in them, shall live in them. Christ has redeemed us from the curse of the law, being made a curse for us: ... "*

*What God Accepts Is Good Enough For Us.'

Living by faith is mixing believing with patience and because of this many fall by the wayside, so to speak.

We discover that one of the hardest pressures to endure is that of waiting a long time. In fact, such waiting does not come naturally to man. It is a fruit of the Spirit called long-suffering or patient endurance.

Allowing God to develop this characteristic in us causes us to have a strong anchor when it comes to times of testing, while at the same time maintaining within us a boldness in our prayer life, We are able to hold steady in God.

Hebrews 10:35-39; *"Cast not away therefore your confidence, which has great recompense of reward. Or you have need of patience, that, after you have done the will of God, you might receive the promise. For yet a little while, and he that shall come will come, and will not tarry. Now the just shall live by faith: but if [any man] draw back, my soul shall have no pleasure in him. But we are not of them who draw back unto perdition; but of them that believe to the saving of the soul."*

"Living in Faith" correctly lays the emphases on the Spiritual side of humankind and does not mean that we become a burden upon the society in which we live. There are those who have used the term 'living by faith' as an excuse for not gaining or indeed desiring to apply themselves to meaningful employment and become therefore a burden upon others. The Scriptures since the very beginning, tells us that God has declared that we should be engaged in meaningful employment, as a necessity.

Among some charismatic and younger believers in particular, it has become a common error – created by either misguided thinking or a lack of correct teaching – especially to think that not needing to work for gain is evidence of greater faith.

The apostles had to deal with such members within their church congregations who were creating trouble through idleness.

The Middle Ages produced many 'Friars' and other pious people who wandered in the streets and lived from the gifts of others. Such an idea is completely foreign to the Bible.

The Church is seen as a community of believers in which individually and separately each one has something to contribute both personally and financially. For a congregation to be sincere in its quest to introduce Jesus to others – particularly the unbeliever – it must beware of false teaching or habits such as those mentioned previously, and therefore be in tune with Godly pursuits rather than selfish ones.

2 Timothy 3:12-17; *"Anyone who wants to live all out for Christ is in for a lot of trouble; there's no getting around it. Unscrupulous con men will continue to exploit the faith. They're as deceived as the people they lead astray.*

As long as they are out there, things can only get worse. But don't let it faze you. Stick with what you learned and believed, sure of the integrity of your teachers – why you took in the sacred Scriptures with your mother's milk!

There's nothing like the written Word of God for showing you the way to salvation through faith in Christ Jesus.

Every part of Scripture is God-breathed and useful one way or another—showing us truth, exposing our rebellion, correcting our mistakes, training us to live God's way. Through the Word we are put together and shaped up for the tasks God has for us."

2 Thessalonians 3:10-13; *"For even when we were with you, this we commanded you, that if any would not work, neither should he eat.*

For we hear that there are some which walk among you disorderly, working not at all, but are busybodies.

Now them that are such we command and exhort by our Lord Jesus Christ, that with quietness they work, and eat their own bread. But you, brethren, be not weary in well doing."

1 Timothy 5:12-13; *"Having damnation, because they have cast off their first faith. And withal they learn [to be] idle, wandering about from house to house; and not only idle, but tattlers also and busybodies, speaking things which they ought not."*

The very nature of faith includes continuance. Once we are persuaded to place our full reliance upon Christ, this reliance grows. Since our faith responds to an objective God, changes occur and continue to occur within us.

The depth and intensity of our persuasion is increased by the working of the Holy Spirit within us. God builds into our character the patience and courage needed to persevere in faith. Faith that only "began" and never went on, may turn out to have only been an emotional stirring.

* 'Biblical Faith Touches The Whole Man And Sets Into Motion A Growth Process.'

The doctrine of continuance in faith is called "perseverance" and is much disputed among theologians. Nevertheless, I found in my early Christian Life that faith is always tied to something. And to understand, from my personal perspective, faith meant for me to learn what it is that God is telling me in my new found spirituality.

Persistence clearly means to persist, to be committed to a thing, to be engaged in a cause, and in all these things be believed in what you believe – not to become doubleminded, so to speak.

I can only write what I believe is God's written Word to me and, considering the following truths which have guided me over the past 47 years of perseverance in 'Living In Faith.'

I respectfully submit those five truths – upon which my faith is based – for your consideration; The title referred to here is my first book released in 2020.

1. God determined before the foundation of the world to save those who believe on Christ and persevere in faith until the end.

   For me this means that it is God's faith in me who He created that enables me to choose to believe in Him and His word for my daily living IN HIM.

2. Christ's redemption is for all, but only those who will believe actually take hold – appropriate – the benefits of salvation.

   For me this means that unless I am prepared to live the life as promised, as well as talk the talk in the practice of all that God, my Creator, instructs me to do, I have not entered into the righteousness decreed by God is mine.

3. Sinful man must be born again and renewed before he can understand, think, will, or do anything God considers good.

   For me, this clearly tells me that what I believe must become a reality in my total life style – not be religion –
   but by my conviction that without Him I can do nothing but IN HIM I can achieve all that My God desires for me to do.

4. Apart from God's grace, man is helpless; but it is up to him (man as an individual) whether or not to respond to God's grace - it is not irresistible.

For me this means that I have a relationship with God through His Son, not by force, but by His Grace alone and that is given to me at Christs expense, through the sacrifice of His life for me. And that this truth is fundamentally mine to choose because I choose to have the faith to believe.

5. Victory over sin becomes available to all who are made partakers of Christ by faith; true believers will be overcomers.

For me it is the evidence of the signs following my believing that gives me the assurance that I am in the Will of God. In my B.C. years I always looked for signs in front of me in whatever field that I, in my sinful nature demanded. But now IN HIM Satan has no hold – no dominion – over me because I am an overcomer in Jesus my Saviour and Lord.

The Bible teaches that Living in Faith is a spontaneous and natural result of faith.

Acts 1:9-14; NKJV. *"Now when He had spoken these things, while they watched, He was taken up, and a cloud received Him out of their sight. And while they looked steadfastly toward heaven as He went up, behold, two men stood by them in white apparel, who also said,*

"Men of Galilee, why do you stand gazing up into heaven? This same Jesus, who was taken up from you into heaven, will so come in like manner as you saw Him go into heaven."

Then they returned to Jerusalem from the mount called Olivet, which is near Jerusalem, a Sabbath day's journey.

And when they had entered, they went up into the upper room where they were staying; Peter, James, John, and Andrew; Philip and Thomas; Bartholomew and Matthew; James the son of Alphaeus and Simon the Zealot; and Judas the son of James.

These all continued with one accord in prayer and supplication, with the women and Mary the mother of Jesus, and with His brothers."

Faith keeps us secure in Christ because it is the conveyor belt, so to speak, which is guaranteed between the Trinity – Godhead – and us who choose to embody ourselves in His security contract – His Word – as a guarantee:

He has already prepared the way, He is the Truth and has embedded in us the Life, all of these things continue to work within us as believers. It is because right relationship – Righteousness – has been restored to us that we are able to have His Faith as our own, due to the fact that we are inheritors of His Kingdom here on the earth.

And this is only possible due to Jesus laying down and giving up his life, and therefore, we need pay attention to the BLOOD OF JESUS poured out for us so that we can live freely in Faith in Him.

1 Peter 1:12-19; NKJV. *"To them it was revealed that, not to themselves, but to us they were ministering the things which now have been reported to you through those who have preached the gospel to you by the Holy Spirit sent from heaven--things which angels desire to look into.*

Therefore, gird up the loins of your mind, be sober, and rest your hope fully upon the grace that is to be brought to you at the revelation of Jesus Christ;
as obedient children, not conforming yourselves to the former lusts, as in your ignorance; but as He who called you is holy, you also be holy in all your conduct, because it is written, "Be holy, for I am holy."

And if you call on the Father, who without partiality judges according to each one's work, conduct yourselves throughout the time of your stay here in fear; knowing that you were not redeemed with corruptible things, like silver or gold, from your aimless conduct received by tradition from your fathers, but with the precious blood of Christ, as of a lamb without blemish and without spot."

Hebrews 9:11-15; NKJV. *"But Christ came as High Priest of the good things to come, with the greater and more perfect tabernacle not made with hands, that is, not of this creation.*

Not with the blood of goats and calves, but with His own blood He entered the Most Holy Place once for all, having obtained eternal redemption.

For if the blood of bulls and goats and the ashes of a heifer, sprinkling the unclean, sanctifies for the purifying of the flesh, how much more shall the blood of Christ,
who through the eternal Spirit offered Himself without spot to God, cleanse your conscience from dead works to serve the living God?

And for this reason, He is the Mediator of the new covenant, by means of death, for the redemption of the transgressions under the first covenant, that those who are called may receive the promise of the eternal inheritance."

The everlasting covenant is the COVENANT – bond-ship – OF PROMISE:

Hebrews 13:20-21; KJV. *"Now the God of peace, which brought again from the dead our Lord Jesus, that great shepherd of the sheep, through the blood of the everlasting covenant,*

Make you perfect in every good work to do his will, working in you that which is well pleasing in his sight, through Jesus Christ; to whom [be] glory for ever and ever. Amen."

Christ's continuing work as our high priest and PERSONAL ADVOCATE

Hebrews 7:21-25; KJV. *"(For those priests were made without an oath; but this with an oath by him that said unto him, The Lord sware and will not repent,*

You [are] a priest for ever after the order of Melchizedek:) By so much was Jesus made a surety of a better testament.

And they truly were many priests, because they were not suffered to continue by reason of death: But this [man], because he continues for ever, has an unchangeable priesthood.

Wherefore he is able also to save them to the uttermost that come unto God by him, seeing he ever lives to make intercession for them."

The earnest of redemption, activates the indwelling Holy Spirit:

Ephesians 1:13-14; KJV. *"In whom you also [trusted], after that you heard the word of truth, the gospel of your salvation: in whom also after that you believed, you were sealed with that holy Spirit of promise, Which is the earnest of our inheritance until the redemption of the purchased possession, unto the praise of his glory."*

The unchanging decree or WORD OF THE LORD:

1 Peter 1:23-25; KJV. *"Being born again, not of corruptible seed, but of incorruptible, by the word of God, which lives and abides for ever.*
For all flesh [is] as grass, and all the glory of man as the flower of grass. The grass withers, and the flower thereof fall away: But the word of the Lord endures for ever. And this is the word which by the gospel is preached unto you."

Our position of being HID IN CHRIST:

Colossians 3:3; *"For you are dead, and your life is hid with Christ in God."*

11 Corinthians 5:17; KJV. *"Therefore, if any man [be] in Christ, [he is] a new creature: old things are passed away; behold, all things are become new."*

God's enduring love freely SHOWN TO US IN CHRIST:

Romans 8:38-39; KJV. *"For I am persuaded, that neither death, nor life, nor angels, nor principalities, nor powers, nor things present, nor things to come, Nor height, nor depth, nor any other creature, shall be able to separate us from the love of God, which is in Christ Jesus our Lord."*

* 'We Can Afford To Put Our Weight On Christ, Allowing Him To Complete The Work Within Us, That He Has Begun.'

Some of the things we must do to CONTINUE IN FAITH:

We must maintain open hearts to the working of the Holy Spirit within us. Therefore, it is absolutely clear that we need to be responsive to the quickening of the Holy Spirit without dragging our heals, so to speak.

If we only go half way in our commitment – total investment – to the Holy Spirit, then we should not expect the fulness of His investment in God's promises, to us.

When we are resolved to accept God's promises through our personal commitment to Him and all that He stands for, then we have what I term the 'EXPECTED ANTICIPATION' to live our life now as if we could already see the things promised for the future.

The Bible gives many examples of such personal investment of faith in God's Word: And I list four Biblical Characters from the Old Testament who have inspired my own quest to have a deeper relationship with Him.

1. Abraham left his secure life in Ur of the Chaldees for a land he had never seen that God promised to his seed.

2. Noah invested 120 years building the ark, when no one had ever seen rain before.

3. Moses refused to remain identified with Egypt but chose to become a part of God's suffering people because he believed God's promise of deliverance.

4. Jeremiah purchased the field of Anathoth immediately after prophesying Judah's 70 years of captivity in Babylon. He believed they would again return to the land according to God's Word. He expressed his confidence by purchasing real estate.

When we apply, the practical virtues given to us through the Godly principle contained in the Bible – God's Personal Letter to us as individual believers – we will most assuredly add to our faith.

Faith is itself one of three cardinal virtues: faith, hope and charity (or love) listed in 1 Corinthians 13:13; But it is also the beginning virtue – that of Faith – which produces Christian character and makes us fruitful rather than barren.

2 Peter 1:3-11; *"Everything that goes into a life of pleasing God has been miraculously given to us by getting to know, personally and intimately, the One who invited us to God. The best invitation we ever received! We were also given absolutely terrific promises to pass on to you—your tickets to participation in the life of God after you turned your back on a world corrupted by lust.*

So don't lose a minute in building on what you've been given, complementing your basic faith with good character, spiritual understanding, alert discipline, passionate patience, reverent wonder, warm friendliness, and generous love, each dimension fitting into and developing the others.

With these qualities active and growing in your lives, no grass will grow under your feet, no day will pass without its reward as you mature in your experience of our Master Jesus. Without these qualities you can't see what's right before you, oblivious that your old sinful life has been wiped off the books.

So, friends, confirm God's invitation to you, his choice of you. Don't put it off; do it now. Do this, and you'll have your life on a firm footing, the streets paved and the way wide open into the eternal kingdom of our Master and Saviour, Jesus Christ."

Chapter Eleven:

"BEGINNING A NEW LIFE IN JESUS:"

John the Baptist was the turning point in prophetic history. The difference John would make to history was so great that it was prophesied centuries before his birth that he would prepare the way for the Messiah.

Luke 3:1-18; KJV. (JOHN'S BAPTISM) *"The word of God came unto John the son of Zacharias in the wilderness. And he came into all the country about Jordan, preaching the baptism of repentance for the remission of sins;*

As it is written in the book of the words of Esaias the prophet, saying, The voice of one crying in the wilderness, Prepare you the way of the Lord, make his paths straight. Every valley shall be filled, and every mountain and hill shall be brought low; and the crooked shall be made straight, and the rough ways [shall be] made smooth; And all flesh shall see the salvation of God.

Then said he to the multitude that came forward to be baptized of him, O generation of vipers, who hath warned you to flee from the wrath to come? Bring forth therefore fruits worthy of repentance, and begin not to say within yourselves,
We have Abraham to [our] father: for I say unto you, That God is able of these stones to raise up children unto Abraham. And now also the axe is laid unto the root of the trees: every tree therefore which brings not forth good fruit is cut down and cast into the fire.

And the people asked him, saying, What shall we do then? He answered and said unto them, He that has two coats, let him impart to him that has none; and he that has meat, let him do likewise.

Then also came publicans to be baptized, and said unto him, Master, what shall we do? And he said unto them, Exact no more than that which is appointed you.

And the soldiers likewise demanded of him, saying, And what shall we do? And he said unto them, Do violence to no man, neither accuse [any] falsely; and be content with your wages.

And as the people were in expectation, and all men mused in their hearts of John, whether he were the Christ, or not; John answered, saying unto [them] all, I indeed baptize you with water; but one mightier than I comes, the latchet of whose shoes I am not worthy to unloose: he shall baptize you with the Holy Ghost and with fire:
*Whose fan [is] in his hand, and he will throughly purge his floor, **and** will gather the wheat into his garner; but the chaff he will burn with fire unquenchable. And many other things in his exhortation preached he unto the people."*

The ministry of John the Baptist is crucial for the understanding of the ministry of the Messiah Jesus, who was shortly to follow him. In fact, the Gospel of Mark, and the coming of John the Baptist, is considered to be "the beginning of the gospel of Jesus Christ...."

Mark 1:1-3; *"The good news of Jesus Christ: the Message begins here, following to the letter, the scroll of the prophet Isaiah. Watch closely: I'm sending my preacher ahead of you; He'll make the road smooth for you. Thunder in the desert! Prepare for God's arrival! Make the road smooth and straight!"*

Until the arrival of John, the Baptist, the Old Covenant prophets had interpreted, confirmed, and applied the law in a moral dimension. But when John, by the commandment of God, introduced the new message of the Kingdom it became a message with an exceptionally large question: "The kingdom is ready, are you?"

John gave a refreshing of the promise in Isaiah's prophetic promise of a voice to prepare the Messiah's way.

Isaiah 40:3-4; KJV. *"The voice of him that cries in the wilderness, Prepare you the way of the LORD, make straight in the desert a highway for our God. Every valley shall be exalted, and every mountain and hill shall be made low: and the crooked shall be made straight, and the rough places plain:"*

And after 400 years of silence, God was again speaking prophetically in Israel. But the message was entirely new. Preparation must be made not only in individual hearts but in society if they are to receive their Messiah. It proclaimed a heralding of a coming King and a new era of Grace which would fulfill all the Law and the Prophets.

John gave and indeed was the proven ministry which fulfilled Malachi's promise of a herald or a forerunner before the Messiah came. This anointing from God gave John a special ability to stir the hearts of the parents and children alike and to lead them to repentance.

Malachi 4:5-6; NKJV. *"Behold, I will send you Elijah the prophet before the coming of the great and dreadful day of the LORD:*
And he will turn the heart of the fathers to the children, and the heart of the children to their fathers, lest I come and strike the earth with a curse."

Luke clearly states that John's Ministry was instrumental in bringing the Old Covenant's dispensation of Law to an end.

Luke 16:16; NKJV. *"The law and the prophets [were] until John: since that time the kingdom of God has been preached, and everyone presses into it."*

The symmetry between John and Jesus was so perfect in that they both preached the same gospel – the good news – of the kingdom. The kingdom is the sphere of God's rule and functions just as God intended – in the beginning – by GRACE.

To enter the Kingdom of God we must prepare ourselves by means of repentance.

* 'If We Believed The Message, Then We Are Obliged To Obey It.'

Matthew 3:2; NKJV. *"And saying, Repent all of you: for the kingdom of heaven is at hand."*

We can understand that John's whole message could be summarized as personal repentance and then to demonstrate personally – never by a form of proxy – our repentance by our obedience to baptism."

In Old Testament times, God was to be found in connection with the Law, the Priesthood, and the Temple, all of which controlled, in an absolute sense, the people. However, God Himself was initiating change. He was doing away with the entire system of Judaism because the entire Law would be fulfilled in the Messiah Himself.

John the Baptised was incredibly determined to present the true nature of the Good News that Jesus was soon to bring to those of that day. Simply put, he told those who would listen, this fundamental truth: In heralding the Messiah – Who was already in their midst – John stated that it was now, that if people who would hear, were then to be open enough to receive Him, they would have to let go of their closed ideas about God. They had to turn their backs on the old in order to receive the new.

John baptized in the River Jordan. This meant that the people had to go outside the sacred city of Jerusalem and be immersed in the muddy old river. John's authority to minister was not from the religious leaders but from God Himself and it was because of this reason the leaders – religious leaders – opposed him.

The conundrum of that day has not changed over the past two thousand years in the religiosity of this current period of man's living.

* 'Religiosity And Churchianity Are Man's Way To Their god.
Christianity Is God's Way For Mankind To Live A Fulfilling Life.'

John 1:33; KJV. *"And I knew him not: but he that sent me to baptize with water, the same said unto me, Upon whom you shall see the Spirit descending, and remaining on him, the same is he which baptizes with the Holy Ghost."*

Not a temporal – relating to worldly or human experiences – but by a Spiritual encounter with God their Creator and Father.

Matthew 21:25-26; KJV. *"The baptism of John, whence, was it? from heaven, or of men? And they reasoned with themselves, saying,*

If we shall say, From heaven; he will say unto us, Why did you not then believe him? But if we shall say, Of men; we fear the people; for all hold John as a prophet."

In this new Baptism people were to demonstrate their repentance of heart by submitting to Baptism differently than that of the Old Testament times. John would not permit the people to go through outward forms. His baptism was different from all the Jewish traditions and rites. People confessed their sins as they entered the water with the understanding that such action entails the breaking from the past.

Luke 3:8-9; KJV. *"Bring forth therefore fruits worthy of repentance, and begin not to say within yourselves, 'We have Abraham for [our] father': for I say unto you, That God is able of these stones to raise up children unto Abraham.*

They exercised faith in the coming of the Messiah. Their sins were remitted – paid for in full and under God's personal guarantee – HIS SON JESUS. But more than this, the axe was laid to the root of sin. - it was a real experience of meeting God.

And now also the axe is laid unto the root of the trees: every tree therefore which brings not forth good fruit is cut down and cast into the fire."

This baptism, which was in itself, a public confession of sin and repentance, separated it from previous forms of baptism and certainly was not seen as a religious ritual. It cost something.

By stepping into the muddy river, you were announcing to everyone that Judaism with its dead forms had not profited you. You were a sinner and needed God to do something on the inside to make you different. You were required not only to verbally confess specific sins to John upon being baptized, but the baptism itself declared that you recognized your whole root to be no good. You wanted God to lay His axe against the cause of sin in you.

* 'Sinners Need God To Do Something On The Inside To Make Them Different.'

Mark 1:4-5; KJV. *"John did baptize in the wilderness and preach the baptism of repentance for the remission of sins. And there went out unto him of all the land of Judaea, and they of Jerusalem, and were all baptized of him in the river of Jordan, confessing their sins."*

Those who entered the waters of baptism with true repentance and faith experienced the benefit of the coming Messiah. People had their sins forgiven when they were baptized. This was in stark contrast to the legal covering of sin available under the Old Testament law given to Moses.

Under the law, sin was remitted through the shedding of blood. The blood of animals such as bulls, goats and lambs provided a covering for a time.

God was looking ahead to the completed redemption that would come via the redeemer Jesus paying the total and absolute price – His blood – so that the sinner could come out from the darkness of sin and come into the glorious Light of God's Grace. Because it was based upon the blood of Jesus Christ Satan lost his hold on the sinner, he was no longer in charge, so to speak, Jesus became the advocate, his blood became the payment, and the sinner has become re-united with his heavenly Father. Just like the prodigal son in the story bearing that name in the gospel of Luke:

But these sacrifices had to repeated again and again. Each new offence required a sacrifice. But Jesus came to offer Himself, the Perfect Lamb once and for all. He was the Sacrifice to end all sacrifices. John's message and baptism pointed toward Christ and focused their expectation upon His work as the Lamb of God.

John 1:29; KJV. *"The next day John saw Jesus coming unto him, and said, Behold the Lamb of God, which takes away the sin of the world."*

John's ministry was traditional in that he wanted to show people that there is a different way than that of the Religion and rituals that controlled all of their lives.

John's message was to create a break with existing Religious way, to break up the strength of religious tradition and to make people ready to hear a fresh message from God.

John was never an end in himself. He knew this. He was always working to direct people beyond himself on to the One coming after him. He was always comparing himself as nothing in the light of the one to whom he gave witness. But even so some people failed to make the transition. When Jesus came, they were still wrapped up in John. Even after John's death we read of his followers and how they had lost what little light they had because they did not walk in it.

John 3:26-28,30; KJV. *"And they came unto John, and said unto him, Rabbi, he that was with you beyond Jordan, to whom you bare witness, behold, the same baptizes, and all [men] come to him. John answered and said, A man can receive nothing, except it be given him from heaven. You yourselves bear me witness, that I said, I am not the Christ, but that I am sent before him. .... He must increase, but I [must] decrease."*

Acts 19:2-4; KJV. *"He said unto them, Have you received the Holy Ghost since you believed? And they said unto him, We have not so much as heard whether there be any Holy Ghost. And he said unto them, Unto what then were you baptized? And they said, Unto John's baptism. Then said Paul, John verily baptized with the baptism of repentance, saying unto the people, that they should believe on him which should come after him, that is, on Christ Jesus."*

Don't lose sight of the truth, the true light of the gospel message is that:

* 'JESUS CHRIST IS THE SON
OF THE LIVING GOD.'

Notice how this movement – those who followed John's message – lost its central message because of their failure to recognize God's change of leadership.

John had emphasized both faith in the coming Messiah and the Baptism of the Holy Spirit. All that remained with John's misguided followers years later was the outward form of John's water baptism. Its meaning was gone. As I write this book 'The Foundations for Christian

Living' in the year 2022 I find that some things, seem to never change!

Since those who wanted to go on to follow Jesus had to be re-baptized – or baptized into His name – what was beneficial in that of John's baptism?

God never asks us to do anything without a good reason. Submission to John did indeed prepare the way of the Lord. Those who allowed the axe to be laid to the root in his baptism were open to the message of the kingdom.

They were not blinded by religious tradition or bound by the fear of their elders. They were already aware of their personal need. For this reason, they could welcome a Saviour who was also a King – one who would tell them how to live their lives.

They already knew to expect something to happen in the waters of baptism. This was no mere rite; it was a meeting with God. When they were told to be baptized in the name of the Messiah after the Holy Spirit proved Jesus resurrection and ascension on the day of Pentecost, they obeyed. John was always making comparisons between his water baptism and the Baptism in the Holy Spirit.

Jesus and His disciples baptized in water, but this was not the emphasis of their ministry. The unique ministry of the Messiah was to pour out the promise of the Father upon those who believed. Those who were immersed in water by John were told to expect the Messiah to immerse

them in the Holy Spirit. The Axe Had Been Laid To The Root In The Water.
>But The Messiah Would Come And Burn All That Needed To Be Purged.'

Luke 3:16-17; KJV *"John answered, saying unto [them] all, I indeed baptize you with water; but one mightier than I comes, the latchet of whose shoes I am not worthy to unloose: he shall baptize you with the Holy Ghost and with fire: Whose fan [is] in his hand, and he will throughly purge his floor, and will gather the wheat into his garner; but the chaff he will burn with fire unquenchable."*

>The key word in John's formula is the word "unto." His ministry was pivotal in the history of salvation. It was the transition between the Old and New Covenants. His baptism pointed those in Israel who would repent and believe toward their true hope:

>>"The Lord Jesus Christ."

Chapter 12:

"FULFILLING ALL RIGHTEOUSNESS"

Mark 1:1-11; KJV. *"The beginning of the gospel of Jesus Christ, the Son of God; As it is written in the prophets, Behold, I send my messenger before your face, which shall prepare your way before you. The voice of one crying in the wilderness, Prepare you the way of the Lord, make his paths straight.*

John did baptize in the wilderness and preach the baptism of repentance for the remission of sins. And there went out unto him of all the land of Judaea, and they of Jerusalem, and were all baptized of him in the river of Jordan, confessing their sins.

And John was clothed with camel's hair, and with a girdle of a skin about his loins; and he did eat locusts and wild honey;

And preached, saying, There comes one mightier than I after me, the latchet of whose shoes I am not worthy to stoop down and unloose. I indeed have baptized you with water: but he shall baptize you with the Holy Ghost.

And it came to pass, in those days, that Jesus came from Nazareth of Galilee, and was baptized of John in Jordan. And straightway coming up out of the water, he saw the heavens opened, and the Spirit like a dove descending upon him: And there came a voice from heaven, [saying], You are my beloved Son, in whom I am well pleased."

Jesus went down to the River Jordan where John was baptizing and presented himself for baptism. He did this at thirty years of age when He realized it was time for Him to begin his public ministry. John had been baptizing only a few months before Jesus came to him. It is clear that Jesus had a deep knowledge of divine destiny regarding this moment of baptism.

John was unsure, indeed to the point of opposition, to Jesus' being baptized by him, for the following reasons:

1: He recognized Jesus as the Son of God, and realized that Jesus, was without sin and therefore knew that Jesus had no need of repentance.

2: He recognized that Jesus had greater authority from God and that the roles of ministry should have been reversed.

Nevertheless, God had a reason for it all and because Jesus insisted that John do it his way, John obeyed. And it was at that moment that Jesus illustrated the full meaning of the phrase to "fulfil all righteousness" (Matthew 3:15).

Matthew 3:10-17; *"What counts is your life. Is it green and blossoming? Because if it's deadwood, it goes on the fire. "I'm baptizing you here in the river, turning your old life in for a kingdom life. The real action comes next:*

The main character in this drama—compared to him I'm a mere stagehand—will ignite the kingdom life within you, a fire within you, the Holy Spirit within you, changing you from the inside out.

He's going to clean house—make a clean sweep of your lives. He'll place everything true in its proper place before God; everything false he'll put out with the trash to be burned."

Jesus then appeared, arriving at the Jordan River from Galilee. He wanted John to baptize him. John objected, "I'm the one who needs to be baptized, not you!" But Jesus insisted. "Do it. God's work, putting things right all these centuries, is coming together right now in this baptism." So, John did it.

The moment Jesus came up out of the baptismal waters, the skies opened up and he saw God's Spirit—it looked like a dove—descending and landing on him. And along with the Spirit, a voice
"This is my Son, chosen and marked by my love, delight of my life."

Jesus came to fulfil all His Father's plans. This included not only fulfilling the Law of Moses but every avenue of obedience to God. Jesus said in His own words that He desired baptism in order to fulfil all righteousness.

There was indeed a kind of baptism among the Jews and that was the requirement of the priests at their consecration, but also note that the process of preparedness for the living as a priest also included the armour which God had provided for them.

Leviticus 8:5-13; "Moses addressed the congregation: 'This is what GOD has commanded to be done.' Moses *brought Aaron and his sons forward and washed them with water.*

He put the tunic on Aaron and tied it around him with a sash. Then he put the robe on him and placed the Ephod on him. He fastened the Ephod with a woven belt, making it snug.

He put the Breastpiece on him and put the Urim and Thummim in the pouch of the Breastpiece.

The question is often asked as to what the meaning or use of the Urin and Thummim are and to what purpose if any they are in today's context? In the biblical account found in the above passage it is not clear as to the meaning. Biblical scholars have suggested that they together represent Light and Truth, Revelation, and Perfection.

Thus, they were to be held close to the heart so that they literally became a part of the whole person. For the priest this became a necessity because the people relied upon them to give Godly wisdom when making decisions on importance.

He placed the turban on his head with the gold plate fixed to the front of it, the holy crown, just as GOD had commanded Moses.

Then Moses took the anointing oil and anointed The Dwelling and everything that was in it, consecrating them. He sprinkled some of the oil on the Altar seven times, anointing the Altar and all its utensils, the Washbasin, and its stand, consecrating them. He poured some of the anointing oil on Aaron's head, anointing him and thus consecrating him.

Moses brought Aaron's sons forward and put tunics on them, belted them with sashes, and put caps on them, just as GOD had commanded Moses."

As Christ was submitted to circumcision (as a child), the initiating ordinance of the Mosaic dispensation, it was necessary He should submit to the initiating ordinance of the Christian dispensation, instituted by the same authority (the Lord God) thus Jesus needed to be washed and anointed for ministry.

John the Baptist identified the Lord Jesus as being spotless, the voice came from Heaven, saying, "This is my beloved Son, in whom I am well pleased."

It was also necessary on another account. Jesus represented the High Priest and furthermore was to be the High Priest over the house of God. Just as the High Priest was initiated into his office by washing and anointing, so also must Christ.

Jesus therefore fulfilled the righteous ordinance of His initiation into the office of the High Priest and was prepared to make an atonement for the sins of the whole of humankind. He was baptized by John (the believer), and anointed by the Holy Ghost, for service.

Jesus had become identified with his people in all things. The term Lamb of God is so original that, if it is historical, it must have its ground in some particular impression which the Baptist had received at the time of his previous meeting with Jesus.

In permitting Himself to be baptized, the Lord Jesus announced to earth and heaven that He was the spotless Son of God, and therefor eligible to die so that we might live. Thus, God pronounce His Son to be spotless without sin or blemish.

When an Israelite came to have himself baptized by John, he began by making a confession of his sins.

Mark 1:4-5; *"John the Baptizer appeared in the wild, preaching a baptism of life-change that leads to forgiveness of sins. People thronged to him from Judea and Jerusalem and, as they confessed their sins, were baptized by him in the Jordan River into a changed life."*

However, there is still a mystery as to what His confession could be, in the light of the fact that He is the sinless Son of God?

I believe the answer can be found in the Prayer of Jesus in John 17: who prayed his prayer on behalf of those in the world who believed in Him, as well as all those throughout the years to come would turn to Him as their Saviour and Lord. This particular Chapter 17 is in fact the "Lord's Prayer. (The common tradition has put the Lord's prayer in Luke 11:1-4; However, this is in fact Jesus response when asked by his disciples, 'Lord teach us to pray.')

John 17:6-26; NKJV. *"I have manifested Your name to the men whom You have given Me out of the world. They were Yours, You gave them to Me, and they have kept Your word. Now they have known that all things which You have given Me are from You. For I have given to them the words which You have given Me; and they have received them, and have known surely that I came forth from You; and they have believed that You sent Me.*

I pray for them. I do not pray for the world but for those whom You have given Me, for they are Yours. And all Mine are Yours, and Yours are Mine, and I am glorified in them.

Now I am no longer in the world, but these are in the world, and I come to You. Holy Father, keep through Your name those whom You have given Me, that they may be one as We are. While I was with them in the world, I kept them in Your name. Those whom You gave Me I have kept; and none of them is lost except the son of perdition, that the Scripture might be fulfilled.

But now I come to You, and these things I speak in the world, that they may have My joy fulfilled in themselves. I have given them Your word; and the world has hated them because they are not of the world, just as I am not of the world.
I do not pray that You should take them out of the world, but that You should keep them from the evil one. They are not of the world, just as I am not of the world.

Sanctify them by Your truth. Your word is truth. As You sent Me into the world, I also have sent them into the world.

And for their sakes I sanctify Myself, that they also may be sanctified by the truth.

"I do not pray for these alone, but also for those who will believe in Me through their word; that they all may be one, as You, Father, are in Me, and I in You; that they also may be one in Us, that the world may believe that You sent Me.

And the glory which You gave Me I have given them, that they may be one just as We are one: I in them, and You in Me; that they may be made perfect in one, and that the world may know that You have sent Me, and have loved them as You have loved Me.
Father, I desire that they also whom You gave Me may be with Me where I am, that they may behold My glory which You have given Me; for You loved Me before the foundation of the world.

O righteous Father! The world has not known You, but I have known You; and these have known that You sent Me. And I have declared to them Your name, and will declare it, that the love with which You loved Me may be in them, and I in them."

As noted above, this Scripture is one of the Lord's personal prayers, and in particular, His concern for the Disciples and those who would be drawn to Him, through their faithfulness.

There are other prayers in the same or at least similar mode to that of Jesus in the Old Testament: A representative collective confession, like that of Daniel and Nehemiah:

Daniel 9: 17-19; KJV. *"Now therefore, O our God, hear the prayer of your servant, and his supplications, and cause your face to shine upon your sanctuary that is desolate, for the Lord's sake.*

O my God, incline your ear, and hear; open your eyes, and behold our desolations, and the city which is called by your name: for we do not present our supplications before you for our righteousness's, but for your great mercies. O Lord, hear; O Lord, forgive; O Lord, hearken and do; defer not, for your own sake, O my God: for your city and your people are called by your name."

Nehemiah 1:5-7; KJV. *"And said, I beseech thee, O LORD God of heaven, the great and terrible God, that keep covenant and mercy for them that love him and observe his commandments: Let your ear now be attentive, and your eyes open, that you may hear the prayer of your servant, which I pray before you now, day and night, for the children of Israel your servants, and confess the sins of the children of Israel, which we have sinned against you: both I and my father's house have sinned. We have dealt very corruptly against you, and have not kept the commandments, nor the statutes, nor the judgments, which you commanded your servant, Moses."*

Jesus then, can be seen as taking upon himself a type of a representation of the sin of Israel and of the world, as it could be traced by the pure being, who was in communion with the perfectly holy God, and at the same time the tenderly loving being, Who, instead of judging His brethren, consecrated Himself to the work of – redeeming – saving them.

Christ fulfilled all of the ordinances of both the Old and the New Testament Covenants. He was circumcised on the eighth day, as was required of all male children under the Abrahamic Covenant. Then, as an adult, ready to assume public leadership,

He brought into being the initiatory ordinance of the New Covenant, inner circumcision through water baptism. Jesus fulfilled all righteousness under the Old Covenant and gave His own body and blood to institute the New Covenant. By these two covenants being brought together in a unity that only the Messiah Himself could accomplish He becomes the bridge from the Old Covenant to the New.

Isaiah 42:5-9; *"GOD's Message, the God who created the cosmos, stretched out the skies, laid out the earth and all that grows from it, Who breathes life into earth's people, makes them alive with his own life:*

"I am GOD. I have called you to live right and well. I have taken responsibility for you, kept you safe. I have set you among my people to bind them to me and provided you as a lighthouse to the nations.

To make a start at bringing people into the open, into light: opening blind eyes, releasing prisoners from dungeons, emptying the dark prisons.

I am GOD. That's my name. I don't franchise my glory, don't endorse the no-god idols. Take note: The earlier predictions of judgment have been fulfilled. I'm announcing the new salvation work. Before it bursts on the scene, I'm telling you all about it."

God first cleanses what He is going to fill with his presence. Each Old Testament priest had to be washed and anointed before he could serve.

This type had to be fulfilled in Christ by His baptism and infilling with the holy Spirit. The same holds true for us.

It is important to recognise that according to the Old Testament it was accepted that lambs used for sacrifice had to be without blemish or fault. They were kept in the house and carefully inspected for defects before they were presented to the priest as a vicarious sacrifice. The sacrifice had to be acceptable. This is precisely what had to be done regarding the final sacrifice, the Lamb that would take away all sin!

Isaiah 52:8-12; *"Voices! Listen! Your scouts are shouting, thunderclap shouts, shouting in joyful unison. They see with their own eyes GOD coming back to Zion. Break into song! Boom it out, ruins of Jerusalem: "GOD has comforted his people! He's redeemed Jerusalem!" GOD has rolled up his sleeves.*

All the nations can see his holy, muscled arm. Everyone, from one end of the earth to the other, sees him at work, doing his salvation work.

Out of here! Out of here! Leave this place! Don't look back. Don't contaminate yourselves with plunder. Just leave but leave clean. Purify yourselves in the process of worship, carrying the holy vessels of GOD.

But you don't have to be in a hurry. You're not running from anybody! GOD is leading you out of here, and the God of Israel is also your rear guard."

The history concerning how Jesus was prepared, scrutinized, and accepted as the perfect Lamb is well documented, both in Scripture and in the secular history of the time in which he lived, because:

* 'If The Sacrifice Was Rejected, The Sinner Would Remain In His Sins.'

The truth, therefore, is that those who desire to enter into His Kingdom must, by faith, be conscious of that factual history, so that they, the Sinner, who has been saved – purchased by such a total price – be prepared to live in the New Creation experience as stated earlier.

And now as we come to the final foundational truth, we need to see and understand the nature of the Shepherd – Jesus our personal Saviour and Lord – Who in His natural life on earth, voluntarily identified himself with the people whom He came to save, therefore, He becomes the Great Shepherd, and we His sheep who are those who have both heard and accepted, not only His presence but also His voice.

Christ was made of woman, under the law for a reason. He became flesh and blood in order to become a true partaker of all that human life is. He further became a Jew, subject to all the law's penalty for sin. At his baptism, Jesus publicly accepted His place as one of the human beings He came to redeem. Through this identification with man, He became able to take our place and die in our stead.

Hebrews 2:14; KJV. *"Forasmuch then as the children are partakers of flesh and blood, he also himself likewise took part of the same; that through death he might destroy him that had the power of death, that is, the devil;"*

Whenever a sacrifice of animals was accepted in the Old Testament, God made this known by consuming that sacrifice with fire. The smoke ascended to him as a 'sweet-smelling savour.' This has been true from the very beginning of man's worship to God. Cain recognized that Abel's sacrifice had been accepted while his had been rejected:

Genesis 4:4; *"Abel also brought an offering, but from the firstborn animals of his herd, choice cuts of meat. GOD liked Abel and his offering,*

However, the New Testament required a fresh start, so to speak, and that of course became the Sacrificial Lamb Jesus.

The Father demonstrated His acceptance of Jesus' offering of himself both as a living sacrifice at the onset of His earthly ministry and as the sacrificial Lamb through death. The Holy Spirit remained upon Him as the abiding fire of acceptance.

We know that The Holy Spirit remained upon Him, from the New Testament testimony of John:

John 1:31-34; KJV. *"And I knew him not: but that he should be made manifest to Israel, therefore am I come baptizing with water.*

And John bare record, saying, I saw the Spirit descending from heaven like a dove, and it abode upon him. And I knew him not: but he that sent me to baptize with water, the same said unto me, Upon whom you shall see the Spirit descending, and remaining on him, the same is he which baptizes with the Holy Ghost. And I saw, and bare record that this is the Son of God."

A vital recognition that John both saw – witnessed – and testified – spoke out what he had seen.

God had given John the Baptist a special sign by which he would recognize the Messiah. He would see the Holy Spirit as a dove descended out of the heavens, light upon a man, and remain there v 33; Until this time, the

Holy Spirit had only come upon men sporadically to anoint them for special tasks. He never had become a permanent resident in a human life before the baptism of Jesus. Here again, Jesus was initiating the New Covenant. Even though Jesus was his cousin, John needed this sign from God to be able to identify Him.

I respectfully say that my story over the past 48 years of Christian service both in the church setting, and in those areas across both Australia in welfare and chaplaincy in the Royal Australian Naval Reserve, and Sri Lanka, where I have had the privileged to serve – in particular amongst a variety of nationalities and cultures – has always had as a foremost intent that of connectivity.

The question uppermost in my mind is 'What would Jesus do in this situation?'

Even now as I type these last few lines of my fifth book 'Foundations of Christian Living' I am constantly questioning the What, How, and When to speak or act according to either His voice or his written instruction and examples seen through the Scriptures.

As the song often sung in the fellowships in which we have ministered: 'Its Such Good News That Jesus Loves Me.'

> It's such Good News that Jesus loves me,
> He came and died that we might Live.
> My heart rejoices, I'm singing Glory.
> It's such good news that Jesus lives.
> Katheryne Thornton; Resource Christian Music No 467.

* 'God Loves The Sinner, But Not The Sin Committed.'

Pastor Barrie.

60 QUOTABLE QUOTES:

1. * 'Keep It Short And Simple.'...
2. * 'Failing To Put Into Practice What We Have Heard From God Is Fooling Ourselves. We Will Have To Give Account Of What We Did With Everything We Heard.' ...
3. * 'When We Have Laid A Solid Foundation, We Can Be Confident That Whatever We Build In God Upon That Foundation Will Stand Steadfast And Sure.' ...
4. * 'The Question Is This: Have We Acknowledged His Right To Rule Over Us? ...
5. * 'True Repentance Includes A Genuine Hatred Of Sin, And A Loathing Of Our Sinful Ways.' ...
6. * 'Repentance Is That Special Moment When We Make The Decision Of Our Will To Turn Around.' ...
7.* 'Repentance Is Our Response To God: Regeneration Is God's Response To Us.'
8* 'This New Life Is The Change From The Kingdom Of Darkness To God's Kingdom Of Light.'
9. * 'It Is From Within, That Sin Arises, And That Is So, Because Of Man's Basic Corruption.' ...
10. * 'Transgression Is Man's Invasion Of Forbidden Territory Or Crossing Over The Moral Boundaries God Has Established.' ...
11. * 'The Most Important Result Of Sin Is That It And Our Fellowship With All That He Created.' ...
12. * 'Gods Word Will Always Bring Light And Life, To Those Who Believe In Him. Satan Will Always Bring Darkness And Death, Because Our Sin, Will Of Its Own, Kind Separate Us From God.'...

13. * 'The Bible is meant to be a personal letter from the heart of the Father (GOD) to the heart of the child of God (ME). And when I respond; it is from the heart of the child (ME) to the heart of my Father (GOD).' ...
14. * 'We Must Lay The Foundation Stone Of Initial Repentance, In Order To Go On Changing, The Rest Of Our Lives.' ...
15. * 'Temptation is not sin itself unless we give in to it.' ...
16. * 'Acknowledgment Of Our Need For Change, Sorrow For Being Unlike God In Character, And Continuing In Repentance.'...
17. * 'Repentance Eliminates Our Inner Deviousness, Enabling Us To Be Direct With God.'...
18. * 'Reformation Deals Only With The Surface; Repentance Is A Change Of Heart.' ...
19. * 'But God Is Always Concerned With The Heart, The Root Of Our Conduct.'...
20. * 'If Our Root Has Been Changed, The Results Will Show In The Fruit Of Our Character.' ...
21. * 'After All It Is Always A Matter Of Choice: Gods Way Or My Way.'

22. * 'Galatians 5:22-23; KJV. "But the Spirit's fruit is love, joy, peace, patience, kindness, goodness, faithfulness, meekness, self-control. There is no law against such things." ...
23. * 'Never My Way But His Way.'...
24. * 'Unless We Depend Upon The Character Of The One Speaking, We cannot rely Upon His Word.'

25. *'Presumption Is Dangerous Because It Pre-Empts – It Runs Ahead Of The Plan Therefore Is Unreliable.' ...
26. * 'Assumption Limits Faith Because It Has No Ownership Other Than What We Think, Not What We Know.' ...
27. * 'Our Heart Response Is Absolutely Essential, For Everything Else Flows Out From Within The Heart.' ...
28. * 'Faith Gives Us A Spiritual Understanding Of All That Is Real.'...
29. * 'We experience a genuine spiritual birth and become new people. It brings us into the realm of the 'CAN DO PEOPLE OF GOD.' ...
30. * 'We Can Love Other Believers. We Can Keep God's Commandments, And We Can Even Overcome The Present World System.' ...
31. * 'Faith Is The Proof Of The Confidence We Have In Him And Therefore His Word.' ...

32. * 'Our Reliance Is Not Upon Our Great Prayers But Upon Our Great God.'
33. * 'Religiosity And Churchianity Were Man's Way To Their God, Whatever That May Be. Christianity Is God's Way For Man To Build A Lasting Relationship With Him Through Jesus His Only Begotten Son.' ...
34. * 'God Gave Us The Law So That We Could Measure Our Own Inability And Therefore, Our Need Of A Saviour.' ...
35. * 'God Has Found No One Righteous, But We Are All Equally In Need Of The Gift Of Righteousness.' ...

36. * 'Justification Means That We Are Legally Declared In Right Standing With God. Explaining This Wonderful Truth Is To Say; Just As If I Had Never Sinned.'
37. * 'One Man Said No To God And Put Many People In The Wrong; One Man Said Yes To God And Put Many In The Right.'...
38. * 'God Can Never Change Or Deny Himself, And It Is Written That His Desire For You And Me Is That We Should Regain Our Status IN HIM Through Believing In His Son Jesus. This We Call The New Creation Life.'...
39. * 'Righteousness Is A Gift From God To Mankind And It Can Only Be Received By Faith.' ...

40. * 'God Loves Me The Sinner But Never The Sin That I Have Continually Committed.' ...
41. * 'Christ Arrives Right On Time To Make This Happen. He Didn't, And Doesn't, Wait For Us To Get Ready.' ...
42. * 'Christ Declared That His Work Was Finished; Therefore, God Continues To Consider It Finished.'
43. * 'God Guarantees Under The New Covenant To Forget Our Sins. Because The Central Purpose Of God's Forgiveness Is To Restore His Fellowship With Man.' ...
44. * 'God Had Determined To Justify Man By Identifying Him With Jesus Christ.'
45. * 'By GRACE - unmerited favour. God's Riches At Christ's Expense.' ...
46. * 'Faith Is Simply Our Outstretched Hand To Receive All Grace Has To Give.'

47. * 'Salvation by faith in grace expresses itself in good works.' ...
48. * 'A Part Of The New Creation Is Being Made Able To Fulfil God's Will.' ...
49. * 'God Will Tolerate No Mixtures. It Is Either Grace Or Law. You Can Add Nothing To Grace.' ...
50. * 'Love Is A Fruit Of Our Union With God. It Is An Outworking Of The New Relationship And We Enter Into That Relationship By Faith.' ...

51. * 'Christian Hope Is An Anticipated Expectation and Is The Reality Of God's Way Not Mine.' ...
52. * 'Christ brought us back, but He also restored our right to share an inheritance in God. He not only set us free, but made us heirs, joint heirs, with Himself.' ...
53. * 'Christ Not Only Bought The Church With His Own Blood But Made Her His Bride.' ...
54. * 'We No Longer Belong To Nobody, Even Ourselves, But We Belong To God.'
55. * 'Yes, To God's Way Means No To Satan, I Choose God's Way. Do You?'
56. * 'BUT THE NOW TIME IS ALL WE HAVE:'
57. * 'Faith, Like Repentance, Is Something We Will Go On Using The Rest Of Our Lives.'
58. * 'What God Accepts Is Good Enough For Us.'
59. * 'If The Sacrifice Was Rejected, The Sinner Would Remain In His Sins.'
60. * 'God Loves The Sinner, But Not The Sin Committed.'

Commendation:

Barrie presents as a man of great integrity and enthusiasm. He is dynamic in his evangelistic endeavours and demonstrates a diverse, flexible yet empathetic disposition. He has great insight and understanding of the vast needs encountered across the many cultures within our nation. He is an encouraging man with a great love for God and His people. He offers many years of experience in teaching, preaching and the sharing of practical biblical principles in churches, community groups and/or organisations and also with individuals who are seeking purpose and fulfilment through relationship building, marriage guidance, all with an ongoing holistic development in an often seemingly difficult life and times. His inspired writings have been instrumental in the releasing of people from despair, depression, grief, drug dependencies, anxiety and much more. It is his heart's desire to assist people through the 'Common-sense Teachings' found in the Scriptures, finding new hope and joy as each individual reaches out in the search for answers to anyone of these needs and more. The Lord has given Barrie an apostolic anointing along with a specific word of encouragement, which in short tells us that "Books are for reading, but without understanding they are just words." In his new role as a 'RE-TYRED MINISTER, Barrie is equipped by the Holy Spirit and ready for God's work and God's people. We commend this book to the reader as an example of the common-sense approach which Barrie brings to those who like reading and understanding the Good News of Jesus and His heavenly Father.   *Noelene D. Rowland-Hornblow*

Barrie J. Rowland-Hornblow.

Born in 1938 in London and never having known his birth parents due to the onset of the 2nd World War, he was raised in a foster-parent family in West Tytherly, a rural village near Salisbury, England. Coming to Australia in 1961 he quickly made Australia his home and has travelled extensively throughout many parts of this very large country.

Coming to 'Know the Lord' in 1975 in Moe Victoria his 'Damascus Road' experience has been a pivotal moment in his life.

Barrie is married to Noelene who has been a co-pastor with him throughout his ministry years since their marriage in 1977. He has a background in the Military (Royal Marines U.K.), Social Welfare (Australia) and Chaplaincy (RANR Australia.).

Pastor Barrie was credentialled within the Christian Revival Crusade C.R.C. in June 1979 ministering in Moe, and Launceston before pioneering new works in Western Australia, over a period of nine years.

He was then invited by Pastor Hal Oxley – the founder of Associated Christian Ministers (A.C.M.) – to join that Christian body of ministers in January 1998 serving in Frankston, Mornington, and Ararat and Stawell and then back to the Latrobe Valley where his Christian service began. Barrie has been the Founder of the Acts 29ers International Ministries since 2005.

He is the Executive director for Associated Christian Ministers International (ACMI) Sri Lanka, where he has established a training ground for indigenous pastors and workers.

Books authored by Ps Barrie include "Living in Faith." – "Our God of Common-sense." – "Living in The Way, The Truth & The Life." – "Walking in the Light of God's Word." - "The Foundations For Christian Living."

www.ingramcontent.com/pod-product-compliance
Lightning Source LLC
Chambersburg PA
CBHW051424290426
44109CB00016B/1418